SKY

is *NOT* the limit

Unleashing A Powerful You

Written and Illustrated by

SANTOSH JOSHI

SKY™

is NOT the limit

Unleashing a Powerful You

SANTOSH JOSHI

Published and Distributed by
SOUND WISDOM
PO Box 310
Shippensburg, PA 17257-0310
717-530-2122
info@soundwisdom.com
www.soundwisdom.com

Previously published by
Embassy Books
120, Great Western Building,
Maharashtra Chamber of Commerce Lane
Fort, Mumbai - 400023, India
First edition 2017, Santosh Joshi

ISBN 13 TP: 978-1-64095-058-0
ISBN 13 eBook: 978-1-64095-059-7

For Worldwide Distribution, Printed in the U.S.A.
1 2 3 4 5 6 / 21 20 19 18

CONTENTS

PREFACE   9

1   WHERE ARE YOU GOING?
     Establish your coordinates   15

2   SUCCESS, SURVIVAL & STRESS
     If you can handle stress, you can handle success   27

3   WELLNESS V/S MADNESS
     Health isn't just absence of disease   51

4   ARE YOU NURTURING A PET?
     Clear your emotional space   69

5   BUILDING BRIDGES
     Treasure your relationships   85

6   SET TO RISE
     Turn setback into a comeback   111

7   BREAKING BARRIERS
     If you believe you can achieve   129

8   DREAM IT, TO GET IT!
     The power of creative visualization   151

9   WHAT MAKES YOUR HEART SING?
     Passion will take you beyond yourselves   167

10   TAPPING THE POWER OF YES AND NOW
     Create magic in your life through affirmations   187

SKY – THE 12 MINUTE MAGIC   201

THANK

Gratitude to you all, who became a part
Of my journey, with your soul and heart

I can't thank enough for what you have been
My support and strength, through all I have seen

You helped me, guided me, through every little bit
And made me realise, that SKY is Not the Limit

To me you are so close, a part of family
A family that spreads, and grows like a tree

Without you being there, it was impossible to fly
To you I dedicate, this book on SKY

YOU

PREFACE

It was a dull Monday afternoon. I had just concluded a workshop the previous day which had almost 50 participants. And like most day-afters, I was just chilling. I like to spend this time after the workshop catching up on the mails and connecting to the, now new set of addition to our SKY family, as we call it. I was glancing through my Facebook page when I noticed a new message. It was from Jyoti Matange, a participant of my SKY workshop (that was held about a month before I received this message). The message read: "SKY Healing has helped me tremendously. I had diabetes earlier but now my blood sugar is surprisingly normal. I am also happier than before! Thanks to you and SKY!"

I was thrilled! Jyoti had been suffering from diabetes for several years. Just before she came for the workshop, she had checked her sugar level and her next appointment was incidentally scheduled after twenty-one days of the workshop. What happened next was nothing less than a miracle. On that 21st day, all of Jyoti's tests came out normal. The doctors were shocked. But Jyoti wasn't. The doctors insisted that Jyoti continue taking her tablets, but she knew that she didn't need them anymore. "I felt so healthy after regularly practicing SKY that I stopped all the tablets. Doctors were worried that it'll come back again but I knew I was going to be fine", Jyoti told me.

Though I was completely sure of the immense potential SKY has, a feedback like this is always very motivating. I thanked the universe again for making me a medium to spread this wonderful technique. The beauty of this technique is, that it is short, effective and uses our body's own mechanism to heal oneself out of the traumas on a physical, emotional and mental level and manifests what you are looking for in your life. SKY has a potential of transforming your life 360 degrees.

I strongly believe that we all are born with limitless potential – potential to heal ourselves, to achieve our dreams, to be successful and reach the top. Some of us are able to realize that potential, unleash it and soar high, while others live in oblivion, getting swayed by the winds of self-doubts, fears, failures, negative emotions and negative belief systems. They spend their entire life struggling to manage their health, wealth, career, and relationships and the stress arising therein. They fail to discover their passion and are scared to even dream big. But it is never too late to begin. History has shown us examples of people who realized their true potential and followed their passion much later in their lives and reached great heights. Once you realize your hidden potential, nothing seems to have the power to stop you from achieving what you are looking for in your life. Even the most challenging situations become your launch pad.

Through this book, I have made an attempt to address all the issues that prevent us from reaching where we are supposed to reach. Through short stories and real life examples, this book will help you reflect on your own life and locate your current co-ordinates. I have also designed worksheets with utmost care and a lot of research, provided at the end of every chapter (except chapter 1 as that is a grounding chapter that makes you get hold of your current position). I urge you to take time after every chapter and solve the worksheets. They will help you bring in the transformation you desire in your life. Following this book will provide you the fuel for you take off from your present location and rocket high in the sky without any limits.

SKY is not the limit drives you to look into your life radically, discover your true passion, unlock your highest potential and start your journey to reach where you truly deserve to be.

SKY, the 12-minute technique I have developed, gives wings to fly smoothly even through the strong pessimistic currents in life. It dispels the internal and external forces that may be pulling you back or swaying you away from your path to your goal. I teach this technique in my workshops. SKY is a serious life changing technique and is best practiced after an initiation from an experienced Teacher, and should be performed correctly to reap maximum benefits. If practiced regularly, it is sure to take you to the next level.

I wish you a life-transforming experience through this book and may SKY be only the beginning of your journey to infinity.

Remember, even, sky is not the limit.

Santosh Joshi
March 2017

PS : I have added few cartoons to break the monotony and convey the point with a dash of humour. Humour helps in reframing the problems that might otherwise seem overwhelming.

You will find that there's a character that is present in all the cartoons and that is a cat. I have named the cat - Cookie. So, 'Cookie, the cat' is wise yet playful, and has an opinion to offer in everything. She is also creative and wonders why the humans fail to see the way she can see things. At the end of each chapter, there is a distilled wisdom in the form of Cookie crumbs.

WHERE ARE YOU GOING?

1

WHERE ARE YOU GOING?

Establish your coordinates

It was raining incessantly that day, flooding all the roads in Mumbai. I had to change my plans and stay back home due to the unexpected rains. I thought of best investing my time in reading the books I had bought the previous day from a road side vendor.

As I picked up a book from my neatly arranged book shelf, a soiled and crumpled paper, fell on the floor. There was something written on it in black ink. Out of curiosity I opened the paper and started reading....

Dear God,   *12th Jan 2010*

Today for the first time my teenage daughter, my princess, screamed at me in front of our family friends during dinner. Her eyes were raging with anger when she shouted and complained about how I was never there for her and then in a fit of rage she said, "I hate you dad, I hate you." On hearing this I froze. It was the most embarrassing moment of my life. Before I could say anything she had left the room. I never thought I would see this day. This has never happened before. Where have I gone wrong? I felt a sharp pain in my heart. I stood there numb, for a long time and realized something was terribly wrong in my life.

She blamed me for many things which I was not even aware of. All these years I relentlessly focused on building my career. I thought this was the only way I could provide everything that my family needed and make them happy. But today I realize that I was wrong. They needed me, and I wasn't there. Am I such a bad father? Do I deserve to hear such painful words from my angel, who I love the most?

God, I have been living like a programmed robot, mechanically moving around in the world of vicious competition. I have been working round the clock, crazily travelling across different time zones. I have not paid attention to my health or happiness. I don't even remember the last time I took a break. My foremost priority was work and only work, because I was convinced that only this can bring the best for me and my family. That one sentence she uttered has dulled all the applauds and achievements of all these years. Suddenly I feel I am alone, though am at the peak of my career. I can see that my wife and my daughter were left far behind, in this race to get to the top. They were longing for my presence, my time and my love and I kept chasing my goals. Didn't realize when we disconnected. I have lost so much in the bargain. Today I feel an emptiness. I realized even I have a heart, when I felt a sharp pain, and I felt like crying. All these years I was only using my mind, and the role of my heart was to pump blood to various organs of my body to keep them going. But today my heart is bleeding and I do 'feel'.

I missed out on so much. My little girl has turned into a beautiful teenager. Where did time fly so quickly? I ignored the feelings and emotions of my wife, who is the love of my life. She has stood by me through everything. I don't remember the last time we spent quality time together. What hurts me now, is that she never complained. I had locked my heart and hidden the keys under heaps of work and my goals, hence I could not see any of these things all these years.

Today, the world sees me as the CEO of a company, successful, making big money, living a rich life. But I feel a vacuum. My health has gone for a toss. My true treasure, my family is far from my reach. I don't get sound sleep and I don't even enjoy a hearty meal. This is not what I had signed for! I am not happy. I don't know what went wrong and when I drifted away. Dear God, I am willing to do anything to get my family back. To hear my daughter say, "Dad, I love you. You are the best Dad in the world!" I can give away my career, my ambition, my money, and everything, I have so pain-stakingly earned; just to hear these words from my sweet little angel. I plead and beg of you to help me regain the lost love in my life, and my life too!

God, I am writing with the hope that you will lead me to find the secret ingredient that will make us a happy family again...

a dejected father

This emotionally charged letter brought tears to my eyes. The dejected father had poured his heart out. He believed that he could provide the best for his family by working hard and earning loads of money. But only when his daughter screamed at him, he realized that only money could not provide for all their needs and make them happy.

Although personal ambition, money and career are undeniably an important part of life, they don't come with a 'happiness guaranteed' tag. As soon as we link our happiness with the amount of money we earn, or the career ladder we climb or our achievements, we are bound to encounter moments when we really start questioning, 'Did I go wrong somewhere?' or 'Am I really happy?' or 'Am I missing something in life?' However, some emotional moments spent by a person with his family and friends can also bring in lot of happiness. Simple things like playing with your child, sharing a meal with the family, buying a gift for someone you love, sharing the good and bad moments of life with your friends or just being there for others; adds great value to life. The father in the letter, was probably oblivious of these simple things and his picture of a happy family came crashing down with his daughter's rage.

I sincerely wish that he has found the secret ingredient already, and they are a happy family again.

Many times, we live a very superficial and pretentious life. Everything seems to be rosy at the surface. But there is a volcano forming inside the crust of life waiting to erupt. This could be in the form of stress, unfulfilled ambitions, sour relationships, bad health etc. Knowingly or unknowingly we ignore the smoke (early signs that something is not right), most often not really knowing how to handle it, and thinking that it will settle down on its own. But finally, the volcano erupts destroying everything around. One of my colleagues in my previous company, was a chain smoker. He was not able to handle stress at work and home and eventually found a respite in smoking. He landed up in a severe cardiac condition soon after.

Sometimes, when we don't address issues in our life or reflect upon the questions such as,

- is everything really fine in my life?

- am I in control of my life?

- or, where am I going?

In all probability, life creates situations where we are pushed to do so.

We cannot deny the fact that, at the core, we are all emotional beings. How much ever we try to pretend to be tough on the surface, every incident in our life, does stir some emotion deep within us. If we don't take cognizance of those, there and then, it gets pushed back, only to manifest later in the form of health issues, relationship issues, or mess up with our work and career. The constant presence of the unresolved negative emotions also produces stress. If this stress prevails for a longer duration, it may lead to depression and become as hazardous as a life-threatening disease.

A stimulating statement by Jim Carrey, the famous Hollywood comedian, astonished his fans, when he said, "I hope everybody could get rich and famous and will have everything they ever dreamed of, so they will know that it's not the answer." We believe that celebrities are superhuman, having achieved name and fame, they cannot ever feel sad. But even after all those achievements, they fall victim to severe depression.

Nobody expected a person like Jim Carrey, 'rich and famous', to be depressed. Moreover, he was a comedian. He always portrayed to be a happy man. But deep within he was crestfallen. It was then, he realized that whatever he

earned could not really make him happy. Being under the watchful eyes of his fans and media, he kept on wearing a mask all the time. Living a pseudo life can itself be very depressing and stressful.

Here I am reminded of a friend who does theatre. He is a fabulous actor and fun to be with. He shared a very close bond with his dad and when his dad passed away, he was sad and bemused. The catastrophe was that the opening show of a comedy play, where he played a lead actor, coincided with the day of his dad's funeral. The show was sold out and could not be called off. He had no choice but to perform even in that situation. The pain he went through was immeasurable.

At times, we are so weighed down by the duties and responsibilities assigned to us that we forget to live. We land up in utter confusion and then start questioning our own self, like the father in the letter. Are we doing what we are, to fulfill our personal ambition or are we doing it for others? The reason could be any. In either case, we need to find what makes us happy. Is our happiness based on how we feel each day, or is it based on our accomplishments and achievements?

There was an interesting blog I read long back, about an Australian nurse Bronnie Ware, who spent several years working in palliative care, caring for patients in the last twelve weeks of their lives. Bronnie Ware writes of the phenomenal clarity of vision that people gain at the end of their lives, and how we might learn from their wisdom. "When questioned about any regrets they had or anything they would do differently," she says, "common themes surfaced again and again." The top five regrets as she witnessed were...

1. I wish I had the courage to live a life true to myself, not the life others expected of me.

2. I wish I hadn't worked so hard.

3. I wish I'd had the courage to express my feelings.

4. I wish I had stayed in touch with my friends.

5. I wish that I had let myself be happier.

This thought certainly made me reflect on my life too. "If I had to die today, what would be my greatest regret?" This question gave me lot of insights into my life. It set me thinking, "where am I going?" and later changed the course of my life. Sometimes when we look at other people, we feel their life is so much better than ours, they are happy and we are not. But trust me, if the universe gave you permission to exchange your problems and challenges with others, you would soon start owning yours.

According to the survey by WHO, it is said that depression has become a global epidemic. One in every five women and one in every ten men is depressed. Why is that so, if the basic nature of our being is 'happiness' than why there is so much despondency?

In the midst of the chaotic life we live, we need to pause, take a stock of our life and ask ourselves these basic questions.

Where am I now?

Am I happy where I am? and

Where am I heading to?

If the answers to these questions are not clear, that means we are living in oblivion. It is a clear indication that it is time to act and change the course of our life. It is time to peel off the mask of 'everything is hunky-dory in my life' and address the issue bang on. By avoiding this, we are cheating ourselves, further complicating our lives. The hardest battle to fight is with our own self.

Each one of deserves to be happy and successful in life. Whether a CEO of a company or a housewife, a student or a labourer, each one of us has the "right to happiness and success", and it is our birthright. We are born to thrive, to succeed, to excel, and to be happy in life. We need to be the sailor of our ship and steer it in a right direction. What we don't realize is that we also have the choice, power and authority to do so.

COOKIE CRUMBS...

IT IS IMPORTANT TO FIND OUT WHERE YOU ARE AND WHERE YOU ARE HEADED TO IN LIFE.

ONLY WHEN YOU KNOW THAT, CAN YOU FIND THE PATH TO REACH YOUR GOAL.

SUCCESS,
SURVIVAL &
STRESS

2

SUCCESS, SURVIVAL & STRESS

If you can handle stress, you can handle success

While I was with a coal trading company, my job was to procure and supply coal from Indonesia, South Africa and Australia, for our customers in the Indian sub-continent. On one such occasion, I sourced the coal from Indonesia which had to be shipped to an Indian customer. I was quite pleased with the deal as there was an on-going requirement from the customer and it had a potential of making big bucks for my company. If everything went well, my promotion was certain with a hefty bonus. During such deals, the quantity of coal runs in metric tons and the commercials in millions of dollars.

I was already in Indonesia to make sure that everything went well as per the plans. The ship was anchored to the shore waiting for the coal to be loaded. But the coal had not arrived. The mine owner informed us about the delay by a day. This was a normal practice, and a day here and there was not so critical. We had to keep the ship anchored at the shore. Three days passed by and still there was no sign of coal. In that situation, my anxiety levels started increasing with every sunset. The ship idly waiting at the shore was amounting to a huge loss. I was on the job desperately trying to put thing to order. There was constant pressure mounting up from my bosses.

After about a week of this taxing situation, the miner expressed his inability to supply the coal. That was the point when I was at the end of my wits. I was helpless. Nothing could be done. As the ship was still resting at the shore, it incurred huge demurrage for the company, as the rent had to be paid on a daily basis. I tried to negotiate with the customer on sharing the losses, but they did not agree. Finally, the demurrage had to be borne by our company. I could see my dreams evaporating in thin air.

Since it was my responsibility, I was under tremendous stress trying to find a way out. It was a situation where there was no escape. I became hysterical. When I remember this incidence, it still gives me goose bumps. Probably I was blessed with a strong heart and the ability to cope up with this insurmountable stress, that I could sail through the highly nerve-wracking situation. While working in the corporate sector, not only does one have to go through stress and anxiety, but sometimes the situation also poses a direct threat to one's credibility.

We all experience stress inducing situations in our lives, when there is no escape. In our daily lives it could be job, relationships, health, finance, children, safety etc. The resultant stresses have become such constant companions that many of us operate with an ever-present feeling of pressure, anxiety or burnout.

The stress can become so unflagging that many people start accepting it as a standard part of their lives. Although we may try to ignore its presence, stress doesn't go away. It just goes to work inside our body.

In today's world, we are living on such a high alert that even a smallest thing like someone not answering a phone call can put us under tremendous pressure.

In 2004, I was in Singapore for our quarterly meet while I was working with a coal mining company. That day particularly, our meeting pulled on till late evening, followed by dinner. I had put my mobile phone on silent mode during the meeting, and forgot to change it later. When I returned to my hotel room, it was almost midnight. I looked at my phone and there were twenty-four missed calls from my wife. I almost froze. My heart started beating rapidly. I immediately called back my wife, hoping and praying that everything was fine on the home front. She picked up the phone after a few attempts of calling. By that time, I had already started sweating in the chilled room.

Finally, when she answered the call, she snapped at me, "Where were you? I called you so many times. I was so worried, when you did not answer my calls. Do you realize the kind of stress you put me through?" She was really mad at me. My wife had casually called, but when I did not answer, the number of calls went up with her rising level of anxiety. Although I was relieved that 'all was well', it took me almost an hour, and a massive phone bill to pacify her.

Though we laugh over that incident now, the amount of stress we went through then, was immeasurable.

I have seen parents become paranoid at the time of their children's exams. One of my friends Kim, developed high blood pressure problem when her son was in the 10th grade. Her son had assured her that he will study well. However, if Kim saw him doing anything other than studies, she would get agitated and her BP would shoot up. Once while she was cooking, she felt dizzy all of a sudden and the next moment she was on the floor. When the doctor examined her, her BP reading was alarmingly high. It had shot up due to the continuous stress she was experiencing.

There is a doctor who had attended one of my SKY workshops. She is a general surgeon, on call for 24 hours. She suffered from anxiety disorder. Her routine was erratic as her presence was required any time in the operation theatre in case of emergency. And every surgery induced high levels of stresses as it was a question of life and death. She would become very anxious in anticipation of the result of the surgery.

In all the above examples, one thing is common. These situations are a part and parcel of our life and cannot be avoided. Then how do we deal with them? To understand this let us look at stress closely. What is it exactly that produces stress? Is it the situation itself, or is it our reaction to the situation that does it?

Stress is usually caused when we feel threatened due to a danger perceived. To understand this concept, let us go back in time when our planet, earth was formed, and life came into being. We lived in caves and jungles amidst other wild animals that posed an obvious threat to our survival. In case of an attack from a predators, we had only two choices, 'to fight' or 'to flight (or run away)'.

'Fight or flight' is the response of our body's mechanism in the advent of danger. We have evolved much since that time. Everything has changed around us. There is no direct threat to our survival now. But our response to danger i.e. 'fight or flight' stayed with us. In modern times, this response gets triggered by simple day to day situations that we perceive as danger.

31

For example, you are going for an important business tour. You are on your way to the airport and unfortunately get stuck in a massive traffic jam. There is no way you can make it to the airport on time and are sure to miss the flight. This thought in the given situation presses the panic button. A threat or danger is perceived by our brain. This triggers the 'fight or flight' response in the body. As soon as this happens, you feel anxious and peculiar changes start taking place on the physical level. Blood pressure rises, more glucose is released in the blood stream, breathing pattern changes, mouth goes dry, palpitations and many more. Your body readies itself for the response to fight or to flight. But in most situations like this, you can neither fight nor flee. This gives rise to what we in modern times call as stress. This response activates several glands in our body, resulting in the release of more than thirty varieties of stress hormones in the blood stream.

These stress hormones if not metabolized over time, leads to many physical, emotional and psychological disorders. On a physical level they give rise to things such as hypertension, imbalance in blood sugar levels, stomach ulcers, decreased bone density, allergies, chronic illnesses, skin disorders, hormonal imbalances; and on emotional and psychological level it manifests in the form of depression, anxiety, anger, lethargy, boredom, insecurities and many more.

In the whole story of 'fight or flight', the problem is the trigger-point, and that is our 'perception of danger'. In case there is a real threat to our life, we need all the extra hormones and energy to take action. Our body's fight or flight mechanism is a wonderful gift given to us for this.

However, in the modern civilized age, we don't find life-threatening situations so often. In today's times, what we perceive as danger are small day to day situations where we feel stuck, such as rush hour traffic, missing a flight, missing a deadline, an argument with a boss or spouse, or bouncing of a cheque, parent in poor health, bad relationship or even children's exam.

This sounds quite common, isn't it? Each one of us goes though at least one such stressful situation in a day. In fact, our life revolves around it. So, in all these stressful situations, our body goes through the same reaction to prepare us to fight or flight. That means, over 30 stress hormones flow in blood stream to relevant organs, on a regular basis. All of this, for events that pose no real threat to our physical survival. And in these situations, we can neither fight nor flee. We just have to deal with it. And dealing with the situation further induces stress.

Stress has become a modern day global epidemic. It completely throws our body out of gear. It is important to guard the stress at the entry level, so that further damage is prevented. But whatever stress and its resultant effects have been accumulated since years, also needs to be addressed.

Manage Stress Before it Manages You

We need to understand that there is nothing which is a problem, it is just a situation that that needs to be dealt with. Each of our responses to stress or a stressful situation varies, and hence there is no universal solution to it. At times, we may feel powerless in the face of stress, but learning to manage stress can spare us of the harmful effects, and prevent us from being a victim to stress. Managing stress involves changing the stress inducing situation when you can, or changing your reaction when you can't change the situation and calming your mind and relaxing. However, the first step is to identify the trigger that produced stress.

Identify the Trigger and Address It

Stress largely occurs due to our resistance to accepting a particular situation or when our expectations are not met with. Identifying a trigger when some major incidence occurs in our life such as a new job, change in location, marriage, divorce or losing someone close, is easy. But finding the source of stress in daily routine is not simple. For example, if you get late for office and you miss the bus, you get stressful; if you have not met your targets and your boss calls for a meeting, you get stressful; if your child falls sick, you get stressful; if you have an argument with someone; you get stressful. Each day will present you with several stressful situations. But these are just the situations, so where is the trigger? The trigger lies in the reaction to the situation and the reaction is based on feelings. In all the above examples the feeling is worry; worry about losing the job, worry about your child's future, worry about losing a relationship.

Worry or anxiety is the projection of a probable result of a particular situation, that may or may not happen. So it is actually non-existential. It may or may not happen. However, it has already done its job – of producing stress. If you pause and question yourself, "What am I worried about? or What is the worst thing that can happen in a situation?", and if you are able to answer these questions, you will have the clarity about the situation, and help you handle your stress. Hence instead of getting stressed, you will be able to address and work on managing the underlying emotions/feelings that produce stress.

Sometimes the trigger for stress also may be a deep rooted belief which could be something like, "I always attract problems in my life". So as soon as you encounter a similar situation, the belief comes to life and stress is produced. Healing of beliefs (as explained in the chapter 'Breaking Barriers') will certainly help in minimizing the stress and its effects.

Never Stress over What You Cannot Control

Many times, we get stressed on the things and situations that are not in our control. Say, you get stuck in a traffic jam. You are late for an important meeting. There are more than a hundred cars ahead of you and as many cars behind. This is a situation which you have no control over. But your immediate reaction is panic and that triggers the 'fight or flight' response. The stress hormones are released and they start working inside. This further escalates the stress and you get stuck in a vicious cycle.

It is difficult to operate from a solution oriented perspective when you are stressed out. For handling a situation, you need to be calm and that is only possible when you manage the stress produced.

One of the many other things you cannot control, is the behavior of other people. But this may cause huge stress. For example, your boss fires you or someone misbehaves with you, or your mother-in-law puts you down. You simply have no control over these things as they are coming from somebody else. What is in your control is not letting those things affect you. Just looking at this situation from a different perspective and not taking them personally may arrest the stress that mounts up.

Stop Focusing on How Stressed You are and Remember How Blessed You are

If you want to live a stress-free and successful life, count your blessings. Even in the midst of a stressful situation, if you shift your focus to what you have instead of what you don't have, you instantly feel peaceful.

For instance, when you are going through a rough financial patch, and you are too stressed about it, look at the people who don't even have the basic necessities of life. This will make you feel grateful for what you have and instantly change your perspective from negative to positive.

In such cases, the situations don't change overnight, but acknowledging the blessings in your life changes your reaction towards it.

Bring Your Focus to the Present Moment

If you observe your thoughts at any given point in time you will notice that most often your mind is rambling either in the dead past or the mystic future. We often get entangled in the guilt and regrets of the past or fears and insecurities of the future (I have dealt with this aspect in my book KEYS). Hence very often we experience worry, anxiety, irritation, anger, fear and all other negative emotions which fall under the umbrella of stress.

It is the most difficult task to control the mind as it loves to wander in the unknown or that which does not exist. It has the capacity to sway us, and our entire being along with it. The best thing to do when you experience stress or agitation, is to be conscious about it and pull the mind to where it ideally should be, by bringing your entire focus in the present moment. Because this is the only moment that exists as past is gone and future is yet to come. If you are able to do this, you can experience your stress dissolving in that moment.

Adopt a Relaxation Technique

This is one of the ways to combat stress. When you are stressed, leave everything that you are doing and choose a quiet place and sit still or lie down. Put on some soothing music if you can. If you are in the office, go to your place and sit on your chair; close your eyes. Take your attention to your breath. Take deep breaths. Feel the breath going in through your nostrils into your lungs and coming back out of your nostrils. Feel the warmth of the breath touching each and every cell of your body and energizing it. With every breath in, take all the positive, rejuvenating energy and with every breath out, feel that all the stress, tension, anxiety, worry is leaving your body. Do this exercise until you feel that your body and mind is completely relaxed.

Once you reach in the space of calm and peace, shower yourself with lot of love. Send love to every cell of your body and feel the cells responding. Convey this message to every cell: "I am in complete control of my situation, and I will handle it from a space of love. All is well in my life"

Repeat it a few times if you like. When you feel that every cell of your body has calmed down, gently rub your palms, rub your eyes and open your eyes with confidence and smile. You will observe that your stress has vanished and you have regained the strength to face any challenging situation.

This relaxation exercise will take not more than a few minutes of your time, and have miraculous effects.

Set up an Anchor

Sometimes when you are experiencing a stressful situation, you become a part of it and you may require some external support to pull you out. This job can be done by your friends or whoever you trust; but they may not be available every time you need them.

So here is an idea to set up an anchor. An anchor is nothing but a stimulant, that acts as your friend who helps you to come out of a stress inducing situation. The anchor is embedded in your sub-conscious mind. So, when you experience a stressful situation, you can bring that anchor to your conscious awareness to dismiss the stress. It could be in the form of an image, sound, colour, shape or symbol.

This can be done through the HOPE (Holding On to Personal Empowerment) technique I teach in my workshops. It goes like this.

Step 1

Sit in a comfortable position and take your attention to your breath. Relax your whole body. Visualize that you are in your favourite place of nature, and experience that place of nature with all your senses. Observe your passing thoughts as they come and go. Visualize yourself sitting on a boulder in nature and soak yourself in the sunrays. As the sunrays penetrate every cell of your body, it attains highest level of relaxation. Slowly you will find your thoughts disappear and your mind becoming calm. This means that you have touched your subconscious mind.

Step 2

When you are completely relaxed, bring out a positive incident from the past that has given you maximum happiness, to your conscious awareness. Re-live the memory of that event, as if it is happening now. Focus on your feelings. Fill your entire body with the positive emotions generated from re-living the memory.

Step 3

At this point bring on your mind's screen an anchor in the form of an image, sound, colour, shape or symbol. Say you have chosen a jingle as an anchor. Give an auto-suggestion that whenever this jingle is played or you sing it, you are filled with the same positive energy. Practice it a few times there. After doing this slowly come back to the present and open your eyes.

The anchor, (the jingle in this case) gets deeply rooted in your subconscious mind. When you encounter a stressful situation next, use your anchor and see yourselves filled with a positive peaceful energy.

Practice SKY

SKY is a 12-minute technique I have developed, that instantly reduces stress. I teach this technique during the SKY workshops.

What most people don't realize is that each one of us has extremely potent healing powers within us, and by using this healing power, we are able to remain healthy and in harmony with ourselves. SKY technique is based on this premise. It has come as an insight during deep meditation, and then worked upon through experiential. The technique combines the stimulation of energy meridians in our body, rhythmic breathing patterns and visualization.

Our breath is a marvelous natural instrument. We can use it to free ourselves from stress, and physical, emotional, and psychological pain. Our breath prevents the upsetting states of mind and body, and helps us to remain blissful, ecstatic, loving, and creative at all times. For instance, when we get stressed, our breathing automatically changes. This automatic response can be changed when a different breathing pattern is adopted which triggers positive thoughts and emotions. Amazing things happens in us when these new breathing patterns become the habit of our system.

How to Create a Stress-free Zone in your life?

"Prevention is better than cure", they say. But can stress really be prevented? Although stress is an automatic response of our nervous system, once you become aware of the trigger and the source of stress, it can be avoided.

Below are the few things if practiced regularly can help you create a stress-free zone in your life.

1. Physical exercise: Any form of physical exercise is good; the only condition being, you should be able to enjoy it. You can simply go for a walk, do yoga or dance on your favourite tunes, go cycling, running, swimming or play any kind of sport. Physical exercise releases endorphins that boost your mood and make you feel good. This will keep your stress at bay.

2. Relax yourself: Learn to relax. We are all running the race not really knowing where we are headed to. In the process, we are always doing something, meeting deadlines, finishing chores, and fulfilling duties. All these things can become overwhelming and stressful. We need to pause from time to time and relax. Understand that the world is not going to stop without you.

3. Have the 'Me-time': Having some time to yourself helps you reflect on your life, know yourself better, gives you the strength to handle the challenges in a more positive way. You can calmly resolve the issue than fret about it. Thus, the resultant stress minimizes.

4. Do what you love: It is very important to do what you love, to follow your passion. It could be music, painting, writing or any other form of art or it could be just helping others or working for a cause. Whatever that gives you happiness. Your job or work may not always be what you love; but if you are able to make some time daily for what gives you happiness and satisfaction; you will be able to handle any stressful situation without getting anxious about it.

5. Always look at the bigger picture: It is said that if there are no ups and downs in life, then you are as good as dead. Life is full of challenging situations; and these situations only help us grow. Stress is only a reaction to that situation. If you look at the bigger picture of life, your problems will seem small and short-lived.

6. Have Faith: There might be a time in your life when you feel engulfed by problems, everything seems to be dark and you can't even see a ray of light. Use faith as a torch to see the way ahead. Remember everything in life happens for a reason. Trust the super power who has created this universe. It is easier said than done, but it still pays to have faith.

7. Believe in Miracles: Adopt this attitude of looking at life with wonderment. The earth rotates on an axis, the sun sets and rises, the trees grow in the forest; aren't these things miracles? The fact that you were conceived out the million possibilities of the gene combinations, grew in your mother's womb for nine months and were born in such a beautiful world; isn't this a miracle? If you look for it, you will see a miracle in each and every small thing in life. Your life itself is a miracle so why worry about anything at all?

8. Believe in Yourself: The best gift you can give yourself, is to believe in yourself. Remember you are an immensely powerful being, having the potential to achieve great heights in life. Problems are just the roadblocks to help you grow. If you believe in yourself, you will never get stressed about anything in life.

9. SKY helps prevent stress: The SKY technique if practiced daily, will not only keep you healthy on an emotional, physical and psychological level, but it will totally eliminate stress from your life.

THE WORKSHEET

Maintain a stress journal. Every night before you sleep, spend at least 10 minutes alone. Reflect on the day spent. Make a note of the following things,

Did you encounter any stress-inducing situation today? If yes, describe it.

....
....
....
....
....

What caused the stress?

....
....
....
....
....

How did you feel emotionally, physically and psychologically? Describe it.

....
....
....
....
....

Why did you feel the way you felt?

....
....
....
....
....

What did you do to handle the stress and its effects?

....
....
....
....
....

Could you have handled it in a different way? If yes, how?

....
....
....
....
....

This exercise will take only 10 minutes of your time, but it will make you aware and conscious of your reaction and your attitude. Once you become aware, you can also change it.

Have a Stress-free kit

You can also have a "Stress – First aid kit" handy. This kit can contain a few magical things that come handy and helps in releasing stress instantly. My stress - First aid kit consists of:

- A cartoon strip in my mobile (I particularly like Beetle Bailey, Hagar the Horrible, Calvin and Hobbes)
- A video of an Animation film in my mobile (My choice is Madagascar, Kungfu panda, Ice age)
- My favourite songs. I either listen to them or I sing aloud.
- Making funny faces. It may sound hilarious but I stand in front of the mirror and face funny faces.
- Leave the room or the place I am in, immediately. Change of place helps.
- Long Walk
- Being with the breath
- Doing something creative (draw a cartoon or sketch or paint)
- Doodling, I love to do this.

Once I am able to pull my mind out of the stressful situation, I am able to look at the whole situation with a different perspective.

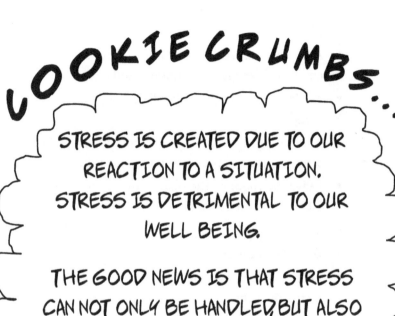

COOKIE CRUMBS...

STRESS IS CREATED DUE TO OUR REACTION TO A SITUATION. STRESS IS DETRIMENTAL TO OUR WELL BEING.

THE GOOD NEWS IS THAT STRESS CAN NOT ONLY BE HANDLED, BUT ALSO MANAGED AND AVOIDED

WELLNESS
V/S
MADNESS

3

WELLNESS V/S MADNESS

Health isn't just absence of disease

During one of my workshops in New Delhi, a participant Rakesh Suri had mentioned about his initiative for street children. Along with a few like-minded people, he had started a computer literacy programme, where underprivileged children were being trained to use computers. I was very inspired by this initiative and decided to meet the children of this school, the next time I was there. That moment came in January, 2014. Before entering the school, Rakesh introduced me to another core member of their team, Arjun Verma.

I was told before this meeting that 70-year-old Arjun Verma, walked with a huge hunchback for several years and needed the support of a walking stick. His health was very fragile and he was always irritable. However, there was one thing that would make Arjun smile, his dream to help destitute children. Arjun had been talking about doing something, but this thought remained a dream for a long time. One day, he decided to follow his dream and with the support of a few people, Computer Shiksha became a reality.

I was happy to hear this story. The only thing I was confused about was the description of Arjun. In front of me stood a healthy, charismatic and charming man, who looked nothing like the description given of an old, fragile, hunchbacked man who could not walk without a stick. That's when Rakesh explained that a few months after they started this initiative, Arjun's life changed drastically. Without any medical treatment or support, he started walking straight. All his health issues vanished. He felt more energetic and enthusiastic towards life. He identifies more with his new self than the man who walked with a hunchback.

Very interesting story indeed. No less than a miracle. How did this happen? Can somebody's physical state be reversed?

Most of the times we ignore our passion and the things that give us maximum happiness in pursuit of the unknown. What we don't realize is, if we don't pursue the things we are passionate about, we create a baggage of self-pity and regrets, which in turn has an effect on our physical health.

My wife was suffering from acidity since a very long time. She had been on antacids for several years. If she did not take the morning tablet, acidity would come with double force. Many advices came her way. She tried to change her lifestyle, food habits, adopted natural remedies but the effect of those were transient. The only change in so many years was from one type of antacid to another. She was desperate to find a permanent cure to this problem.

I took an appointment with the best doctor in town with a reference from a doctor friend. After examination the doctor advised a number of tests including endoscopy. Then on a friendly note he got chatting, "acidity is a very misused term. Our body produces acid for digestion. In that regard, each one of us has acidity. I will tell you a very interesting fact." He continued, "a few decades back, when the sophisticated medical equipments were not available, we used to perform a procedure called Vagotomy on a patient suffering from gastric ulcers. There is a Vagus nerve that goes from our brain stem to the abdomen that controls the digestion of food. During this procedure we cut that nerve." This gripped my attention.

"In case of anxiety, anger or any kind of intense emotion or stress, our energy gets depleted and our body prepares itself for the replenishment of this energy by producing more acid in anticipation of food. This acid if unused produces reflux and gastric ulcers. By cutting the Vagus nerve, this signal does not reach the stomach and the resultant effect is avoided", he added.

The doctor had hit the nail on the head. It has been more than a few years now, my wife came out of this vicious cycle of antacids by mentally performing Vagotomy.

It is simply amazing the way our body and mind work in unison.

Understanding Health & Healing

The build of the modern world is such that most people are fixated on their physical health but completely ignore every other aspect of well-being. People eat and drink the right things, work out regularly and consult their doctor for the slightest physical problem, yet they manage to fall ill. Why does that happen? The reason being, the state of our physical body is not the best parameter to judge our health. World Health Organization (WHO) describes health as "a state of complete physical, mental and social well-being and not merely the absence of disease or infirmity."

According to me, there are two more aspects to health – emotional and spiritual well-being. A healthy person is one who is complete and whole in all these five aspects; which I call the "Health Pyramid".

1. Physical
2. Emotional
3. Mental
4. Social and
5. Spiritual

These five aspects are intertwined and an imbalance in any one causes a setback in health. Similarly one aspect can also help other to stay healthy. For example, a person diagnosed with depression or anxiety is most often advised some form of physical activity apart from taking medication. This is because, the body produces hormones known as endorphins which improve mood and relieve stress. Depression can be alleviated by improving mood and anxiety can be relieved by reducing stress.

Physical Health

The first and largely understood aspect is physical health which is maintained with proper nutrition, hygiene and

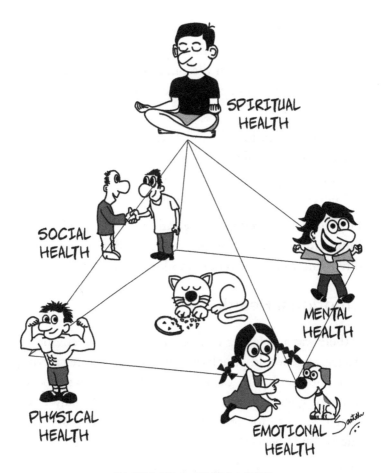

SPIRITUAL
HEALTH

SOCIAL
HEALTH

MENTAL
HEALTH

PHYSICAL
HEALTH

EMOTIONAL
HEALTH

HEALTH PYRAMID

exercise. We can say we are physically healthy if all our organs are working in perfect condition and they are in sync with each other.

A few years back there was a news that one of the youngest CEOs of a multi-national company succumbed to a massive stroke. A lot has been talked about the stresses, deadlines and the ruthless competition in the corporate environment today. But what baffled everyone was that a fitness freak who was in the pink of his health suffered a stroke at such a young age. The reason that came forth was, lack of sleep.

One has to work long hours, drive through endless traffic jams and juggle difficult relationships at home and at work. All these things leave no room for personal recreation and self development as the mind is always on an overdrive.

Having gone through the grind myself, I realize how important it is to remain physically fit. But what all of us often tend to neglect is our emotional health.

Emotional Health

If there was a weighing machine to measure the emotional baggage, we would be aghast at the weight we are carrying that is beyond your capacity. This baggage could be in terms of guilt, regret, anger, resentment and many more which we carry for years, not realizing that it is affecting our health in general.

During my sessions, I use a tool called 'regression therapy' to address this issue. Through this therapy, we go back in time in our past and relieve the memories that have caused emotional traumas. The most common question asked to me is, "when you say that one must live in the present moment, why does one need to go to the past?" I reciprocate with another question, "How much can you walk easily without getting tired? May be four to five kilometers. Now if I load you with a bag of say 50 kg, how much would you be able to walk? May be a kilometer with a lot of effort?" Similarly we are all walking with a huge load on our back from the past that is weighing us down. It is of utmost importance to let go of that emotional baggage so that we can call ourselves healthy.

I know of a 40-year-old gym instructor who died of a heart attack. He had a six-pack body, and he was very particular about his diet and exercise regime. All the people who knew him were shocked about this news. Later I learnt that he had a couple of broken relationships and he was very disturbed emotionally.

Emotional health which is the most neglected aspect of health, depends on the emotions we experience and how far we let them rule us. When we encounter an emotion such as anger, regret, guilt, fear, we try to suppress it, probably not knowing how to handle it. There are situations in our life like broken relationships, not raising up to the expectations of self and others, or victim to the circumstances, wherein lot of negative emotions are generated. These push us on a downward negative spiral, finally landing in depression.

The most powerful tool to stay emotionally healthy is to practice forgiveness, letting go, and gratitude. Letting go will not happen unless we forgive, and forgiveness is the most difficult thing to do. For example, someone has cheated on you and you are badly hurt; it is not easy to forgive that person. When you encounter that person again, that emotion in you gets triggered and the anger and other negative emotions gush out at the very first chance. So how does one forgive? As long as we consider the other person to be a culprit, it is impossible to forgive. But as soon as we change the perspective of looking at it and consider being in the shoes of the other person and look at the divinity in him, forgiveness will come naturally.

Another powerful tool is Gratitude. If we are grateful for every small thing in our life, we will always be emotionally fit, happy and healthy.

Mental Health

Mental health depends on one's attitude, right thoughts and passion. It is commonly said "attitude is more important than aptitude." Sometimes the journey to our goal gets tough. There are really challenging times. To cope up with these one needs a sound mind or mental health. One of my acquaintances had passionately started a business with all the positivity and faith. But there were a few failures after the initial honeymoon period. Unable to cope up with those failures, he took to heavy drinking and smoking and landed up in hospital with a liver failure.

Mental health can be cultivated through positive thoughts, being in the company of positive people, reading inspirational books and biographies and so on. But most importantly we need to change our perspective towards life. For example, failure can be looked at as a stepping stone to success rather than the end of the world. Only the change of attitude can change over the game of life in your favour.

Social Health

An often ignored aspect is social health which is dependent on giving back to society, helping others and leaving a legacy. The example of Arjun Verma mentioned above is a real example of how healing takes place. All Arjun needed to do was give back to society or balance his social health. The law is indeed true – "whatever we give others, nature gives us back in manifolds." Teaching computers to little children not only improved his overall health but also gave him joy, peace and inner satisfaction.

Humans are social beings. We have an inherent need to be with people and interact with them. However in the age of internet where we are connected electronically, being in the virtual world all the time, we miss on the real time connections. We need to make an effort to prioritize this important aspect of our life.

Spiritual Health

The significance of the spiritual health is often understated. It is the binding factor between all the five aspects. This can be understood easily if compared to a pyramid. A pyramid is said to be one of the more stable structures. But this stability depends on the five vertices. Our health too, depends on five vertices – physical health, emotional health, mental health and social health being the bottom ones and spiritual health, the top. The bottom four vertices may seem the most important but without the top vertex, the structure will have no shape. Similarly, spirituality is the guiding force and it holds the other four aspects of health, thus giving stability to the structure.

Spirituality is often confused with religion or faith. In fact, spirituality is just a way of life. It is all about knowing oneself, understanding the greater purpose of one's existence, and bringing one's mind body and soul in harmony. It can be achieved through calming the mind, raising the consciousness and igniting the spirit. One of the tools to do this is through yoga and meditation.

Only when you are able to build this pyramid can you truly call yourselves healthy.

THE WORKSHEET

Being healthy is not a goal; it's a way of life. The time you take to reach your destination completely depends on how stable your health pyramid is. Understanding your current health status is a key part of building a sustainable health pyramid.

The following exercise will help you know where exactly you stand in every aspect of your health. Be sure to truthfully answer the questions. This test is not about how you feel currently, but how you feel consistently. Therefore, don't base your answers on how you feel now, but rate it as an average of how you felt for last few weeks.

When you do this exercise, you need to do a lot of introspection, contemplation and analysis; hence find a quiet place where you can give your full focus, where there is no noise, cell phones or any other distractions.

Remember health is wealth; and there is nothing greater than health. So get ready and assess how healthy you are.

Physical Health

Do you feel lethargic when you wake up in the morning?

N Y ....

Do you often see yourself complaining about some discomfort in your body?

N Y ....

Do you have pains and aches in your body most often?

N Y ....

Do you think your appetite is above or below normal?

[N] [Y] ....

Is your weight above or below normal for your age and height?

[N] [Y] ....

Emotional Health

Do you feel emotionally drained all the time?

[N] [Y] ....

Do you often see yourself having guilts or regrets about your past?

[N] [Y] ....

Do you live in fears and insecurities about your future?

[N] [Y] ....

Do you find difficulty in expressing your emotions and reacting to situations?

[N] [Y] ....

Are there a lot of unresolved issues in your life?

[N] [Y] ....

Psychological Health

Do you have problems in focusing on a task in hand?

☐ N ☐ Y ....

Do you get anxious when you have to meet the deadlines?

☐ N ☐ Y ....

Do you find difficulty in prioritizing things?

☐ N ☐ Y ....

Do you have a difficulty saying 'No'?

☐ N ☐ Y ....

Do you often experience loss of memory?

☐ N ☐ Y ....

Social Health

Do you often shy away from people?

☐ N ☐ Y ....

When someone comes forth to help you, do you doubt their intentions?

☐ N ☐ Y ....

Are your relationships transient?

☐ N ☐ Y ....

Do you think socializing is a complete waste of time?

☐ N ☐ Y ....

Do you think, "leaving a legacy" is a farce?

☐ N ☐ Y ....

Spiritual Health

Do you think meditation is the job of older people?

☐ N ☐ Y ....

Do you connect spirituality with religion?

☐ N ☐ Y ....

Do you believe that only material things can bring you real joy?

☐ N ☐ Y ....

Do you feel that compromising your principles to achieve something is okay?

☐ N ☐ Y ....

Do you think spirituality is an over-hyped term?

☐ N ☐ Y ....

Please Note: If the answers to all the questions are NO, then you can call yourself a healthy person. If the answer is a YES to any of the questions, I urge you to ponder upon that question and make notes on why you think so. The more you introspect, the more you gain clarity about your life.

ARE YOU NURTURING A PET?

4

ARE YOU NURTURING
A PET?

Clear your emotional space

Few years back, when I was on a vacation to a place which is about 200km from Mumbai, I had an amazing experience. We had booked ourselves in a quaint country cottage that was located on the top of the hill. It was surrounded by valleys as deep as they were wide, sitting happily in the laps of mountains covered with rugs of trees, green, yellow and scarlet; rivers and lakes. It was one of the most picturesque locations I had ever been to; the most ideal kind of place for unwinding.

As I stood in the balcony of my room, drowning myself in the mesmerizing view, I felt the soft gentle breeze caress my face. Even the sound of the breeze was so clear! In fact, the only sound there, was of that breeze, occasional rustling of leaves and chirping of birds. As we drew closer to the evening, the setting sun's rays in a mixture of red and orange hues lit up the sky over the horizon. It was a spellbinding sight that is hard to describe within the boundaries of words.

As I stood there, I could experience an extreme sense of calm and bliss, and could hear my own voice talking to me. I could connect to my deeper self and the nature around me with ease. 'Where had this voice, peace and calm disappeared?' I thought. How I wished I could remain in that tranquil spot for ever.

This usually happens when we visit a place of nature. Along with the decrease in the environmental pollution, there is a decrease in PET as well. You get a chance to be with yourself in true sense.

What is PET?

Do any of the following resonate with you?

- You ask someone, "Is there anything wrong?" and you get an abrupt reply, "No! everything is fine." But you sense that there is something wrong.

- Your boss is upset and comes and slams a file on your table. You think, "Why does he have to be rude to me?" and you feel offended and irritated.

- You are in a company of a person who is particularly in a bad mood and your mood turns sour at the end of the meeting.

This happens with us on a day-to-day basis. But how do somebody else's emotions rub on to us and why do we get affected by them?

To understand this let us look at our own selves. Experts say, on an average, a person has around 50,000 to 70,000 thoughts per day. The thoughts give rise to emotions and they together control the frequencies of the brainwaves that are emitted by our brains. These frequencies change with our thoughts. The result has an influence on our body language as well.

Each one of us is continuously emitting brainwaves of different frequencies, depending on our thought patterns, situations, circumstances, and our mental, emotional and physical state.

Imagine you are in a room filled with 1,000 people, and all are thinking different thoughts and subsequently emitting different brain waves. If a picture is taken of these waves it will be nothing less than a chaos.

You must have also observed that when you are in a crowd, you feel confused and are unable to think clearly. Why does this happen? These waves affect us at a subconscious level. If most of the thoughts are negative, which means worry, anxiety, insecurity; then even a positive person is likely to get affected and experience a change in his state of mind. On the other hand, if you enter a place of worship or are amid people with positive thoughts, your thinking can change from negative to positive. This is what I call as PET - Pollution of Emotions and Thoughts. The PET is more during the day than in the wee hours of morning and at late nights.

I still remember, in the year 2000, when I was hunting for a house in Mumbai, the broker showed us many houses. But I distinctly remember going to one house, where there was an old man who was paralytic, frail and had no will

to live. The other members of the family were also visibly depressed. As soon as I entered that house, I had a strong urge to run away from there. But since the broker was my friend and I did not want to offend him, I looked through the whole house. But when I came out, my mood had changed completely. Suddenly I felt drained, irritable and sad. I had to drop all other plans and rush back home. When the space you are in, is infected by negative emotions and thoughts, you can easily get affected, especially if you are an 'empath'.

Who is an Empath?

An empath is a person with an innate ability to sense and perceive the mental and emotional state of the people around or the energies in an environment. If you are an empath, you can easily sense the stress, anxiety, fear from other people. You not only sense them but also draw those feeling inside your body as your own. It may not be from the people you love or hate or you have any emotional connect with; but you could also be impacted by strangers.

For instance, if you are around someone who is angry, you feel that anger without that person ever saying a word. Or if you are around a person who is very happy, you start feeling happy without any conversation.

Marco Iacoboni, a neuroscientist at the University of California at Los Angeles, is best known for his work on mirror neurons. He explains this phenomenon quite convincingly. Iacoboni says, "What do we do when we interact? We use our body to communicate our intentions and our feelings. The gestures, facial expressions, body postures we make are social signals, ways of communicating with one another. Mirror neurons are the only brain cells we know of that seem specialized to code the actions of other people and also our own actions. They are obviously essential brain cells for social interactions. Without them, we would likely be blind to the actions, intentions and emotions of other people. The way mirror neurons likely let us understand others is by providing some kind of inner imitation of the actions of other people, which in turn leads us to 'simulate' the intentions and emotions associated with those actions. When I see you smiling, my mirror neurons for smiling fire up too, initiating a cascade of neural activity that evokes the feeling we typically associate with a smile. I don't need to make any inference on what you are feeling, I experience immediately and effortlessly (in a milder form, of course) what you are experiencing."

We cannot discount the fact that we are all emotional and social beings and to that effect we are all empaths to some extent. Hence most of us get affected by PET, although we may not realize it consciously. It can be highly draining and exhaustive, setting you on an emotional spiral.

However, empaths can be good healers if they know how to guard themselves from the negative emotions.

Constant Complaining Rewires Your Brain

There was an interesting research I came across while I was surfing on the internet. Complaining about things around comes very naturally to us. We have certain expectations about how things should work, how people should behave and so on. When these expectations are not met, we switch to a complaining mode. For instance, "He drives too fast.", "She talks too much", "He never does anything on time.", "My boss is highly dominating", "My son doesn't study", and so on. All these statements and more have become a natural part of our daily conversations. If you carefully observe your conversations, you will notice how frequently you are complaining.

How does complaining affect us? It affects as much as smoking or eating junk food would, or even more. You feel good when doing it, but it causes severe damage to your body in the long run.

Our brain loves efficiency; so when a behaviour is repeated, the neurons branch out to each other for an easy and efficient flow of information. This is what happens when you are complaining too. After a while you don't even realize that you are complaining.

Research from Stanford University has shown that complaining shrinks the hippocampus, an area of the brain that's critical to problem solving and intelligent thought. Damage to the hippocampus is scary, especially when you consider that it's one of the primary brain areas destroyed by Alzheimer's.

Well, the damage does not stop here. Constant complaining releases cortisol which is a stress hormone in the body. This further creates a fight or flight response, giving rise to several health issues. (Discussed in detail in the chapter of Success, Survival and Stress)

Complaining or any negative thought is a silent-killer. It not only affects you but also those around you by causing PET.

Emotional Spiral

You will be really amazed at how a very simple negative or positive feeling can take us up or down the emotional spiral.

Let us look at the negative emotional spiral. For example, one day you get a thought, "I am feeling bored today." This gives rise to another thought, "There is nothing right in my life" to "I am unable to live the life I want" to "I am not sure whether I will be ever able to do anything worthwhile with my life" to "I hate the situation I am in and the people around me" to "I will be left far behind everybody" to "I don't even know why I am alive. I have no right to live. I am a burden on this planet". This is how the spiral works. From the state of boredom, to pessimism, frustration, doubt, worry, anger, insecurity, unworthiness eventually leading to depression.

It is important to break the spiral right at the first step. If you feel bored, don't stay in the state of boredom, go out, do something creative, anything that will take you out of boredom and prevent the avalanche of negative emotions that follow. If handled at the right moment this negative emotional spiral can be converted to a positive one.

May be you could say, "Although I am feeling bored, what can I do to make a difference?" This will set you on a positive emotional spiral. It will bring in optimism, enthusiasm, passion, love, freedom, empowerment, and joy.

Once you ride on the positive emotional spiral, you create a strong positive energy field around you, that prevents you from getting affected by the PET.

Everybody's emotions vary throughout the day depending on lot of factors. If you allow our happiness to be dependent on how other people around you feel, you are in for a roller-coaster ride, and a bumpy one indeed.

Is it possible to come off the roller-coaster ride? Is it possible to not get affected by PET? It is possible to not get sucked into other people's emotions?

Certainly Yes...!

The following can keep you from getting affected:

Observe Your thoughts

Being conscious in every moment certainly helps to live a better life. If you are an observer to the thoughts that are passing through your mind, you are also able to handle those. Whenever you catch yourself of a negative thought, stop there and address it. Realize that it is going to do you only harm and no good. Immediately change it to positive thought. Especially if you are in a zone infected by PET, being conscious about your thoughts will help.

Leave the space affected by PET immediately

Sometimes suddenly, you may start feeling low, irritable, frustrated, depressed or drained, without any apparent reason. Be sure, that the space you are in is being infected by PET. The best thing to do at such times is walk out of that space and go for a nature walk. Nature has the ability to absorb all the negative thoughts that we carry.

Wear a protective shield

I find this technique very useful. Sit in a comfortable position with your eyes closed and focus on your breathing. Visualize a pillar of bright white light descending from the sky and covering your whole body. Let it continue for a few minutes. Then affirm, "I am divinely guided and protected". Try it. This simple technique works wonders.

THE WORKSHEET

It is important to know how emotionally vulnerable you are. Answer the following questions in either 'Y' for yes or 'N' for no. If you wish, you may write a comment in the space provided, as to why you think so. If more than 50% of your answers are a Yes, then you are an empath and you are most likely to get affected by PET. Once you know where you stand, you can take appropriate action to guard yourself from PET.

1. Feel or sense the energy of a particular place, people or things.

$\boxed{N}$ $\boxed{Y}$ ....

2. You often develop a headache or become irritable or feel drained when you are in a crowd.

$\boxed{N}$ $\boxed{Y}$ ....

3. Your happiness is dependent on other people's happiness.

$\boxed{N}$ $\boxed{Y}$ ....

4. You get affected by violent, tragedy or horror movies.

$\boxed{N}$ $\boxed{Y}$ ....

5. You find yourself becoming an 'agony aunt' for people around you.

N Y ....

6. You catch a lie easily.

N Y ....

7. You can make out the genuineness and intentions of people in the very first meeting.

N Y ....

8. When you see somebody hurt physically, you also feel the pain.

N Y ....

9. You often feel the need for 'alone time'.

N Y ....

10. You often get emotionally disturbed.

N Y ....

11. You often find yourself sacrificing a lot for others.

N Y ....

12. You are intuitive.

[N] [Y] ....

13. You can read people's minds.

[N] [Y] ....

14. You go through extreme emotional highs and lows, sometimes without any logical reason.

[N] [Y] ....

15. You think you can become a good healer.

[N] [Y] ....

16. Your heart reaches out to people who are mentally and emotionally weak.

[N] [Y] ....

COOKIE CRUMBS...

CONSTANT NEGATIVE DIALOGUE WITH SELF AND OTHERS CREATES A NEGATIVE ENERGY FIELD AROUND YOU AFFECTING YOU AND THE PEOPLE AROUND YOU.

TO GET IN TOUCH WITH YOUR INNER CORE, AND TO BE ABLE TO UNLEASH THE POWERFUL YOU, YOU NEED TO GUARD YOURSELF AGAINST THE PET.

BUILDING
BRIDGES

5

BUILDING BRIDGES

Treasure your relationships

In the beginning of my career as an engineer, my first job was on the shop floor of a steel plant as a graduate engineer trainee. There were about 1200 employees working there. We all lived in a beautiful township constructed around the steel plant, far away from the city, like a big close-knit family. The person in charge of the plant was Mr. Singhal. It was a challenging task to manage such a huge plant and so many people, but our boss Mr. Singhal executed his role to perfection. He and his family were always there to support, encourage, and cheer everyone around them.

We were a bunch of young enthusiasts, just out of college, set on the path to achieve our dreams. The relationship we shared with our boss was unique; on one hand, he drove us to perform at our peak by being a strict boss, while on the other, he was a confidant with whom we shared our life issues over a glass of beer. He was our friend, philosopher and guide in the true sense.

Once we had some foreign visitors to our plant. They were impressed by the impeccable way the plant was operating.

I was present there, when one of them asked, "Mr. Singhal, how do you manage such a huge steel plant so well?"

To which he replied, "Where do I manage the plant?"

Looking at their puzzled faces, he quickly added with a gentle and reassuring smile, "I don't manage the plant, I only manage people. They do the rest."

This was one of the most profound lessons I learnt during the early part of my career, which helped me enormously in my life.

Recently, I had an opportunity to conduct the SKY corporate workshop for the same organisation. It was a nostalgic moment for me. I visited the plant after more than twenty years. Mr Singhal had retired long back, however few of my ex-colleagues were still there. Many new young graduates had joined. Some new buildings had come up in the complex. Lot of things had changed superficially, but the legacy left by Mr. Singhal was intact. I could feel the same sense of belonging to this place, as I had felt twenty years back. There was a reference of Mr. Singhal in almost all the conversations I had with my ex-colleagues. I was surprised that most of the new employees also knew him though they had never worked with him.

This is the power of building relationships. It not only helps take the organisation to the next level, but also creates an everlasting impact on people's minds and a sweet taste in their hearts, forever.

Building relationships is the basic and the most important part of any business or profession, but unfortunately we are not academically trained for it.

It is said that you may not remember what was said to you but you will never forget how it made you feel.

Lately I visited my bank to complete some formalities. I was waiting there, as my relationship manager was getting my papers ready. I like to observe people around me, when I am not doing anything. I believe that our life experiences and the people around us are our greatest teachers.

On the other desk, I saw an old gentleman probably in his 70s patiently waiting, as the bank officer was trying to sort out some issues related to his account. Our eyes met and we exchanged smiles. After a while, I heard an argument between the officer and the old man. When the officer could not find a satisfactory solution to his problem, the branch manager who was observing this from her glass cabin, stepped in.

Introducing herself, she said, "Sir why don't you switch to online banking to avoid all these hassles?"

"You see Ma'am; I am an old man. I don't understand this online stuff" he replied politely.

"Oh, it's very easy Sir. My father who is 75-year-old, also uses it."

This statement apparently offended the old man. He snapped at her, "Madam, your father must be an intelligent man...I am not!".

As much as we agree on the professionalism at work we must not forget that after all we are emotional beings. Emotions come from heart, not from mind. And the language of the heart is love, care and kindness. In any business, when you show your customer or client that you care for them, you have won them over; then what remains is mere formality. Just as we have a basic need for food, clothing and shelter, we have an inherent need for good relationships in life and relationships are nurtured in the domain of heart.

The success and quality of your life depends a great deal on the quality of relationships you share with people around you. I recently met an old man who worked very hard throughout his life and made a lot of money. He was cheated by his brother in business and was left bankrupt. So 'earning money' became the mission of his life. Now he is retired and lives with his family in a luxurious duplex in a plush neighbourhood. His wife passed away a few years back and his children and grand-children are busy with their own lives. He looked depressed, when I met him. He said, "You know, the biggest regret I now have is, that I did not cultivate good relationships. My entire life revolved around earning money. I had no time for my friends and family all the while. Now when I need them, there is nobody around. I am living in best house with all the luxuries, but I can't tell you how lonely I feel."

Good relationships are an investment of lifetime; you can reap the dividends at the time you need them the most. But you need to work toward building and nurturing them. Cultivating relationships is an art and some people are naturally blessed with it. Nevertheless, it can also be learnt.

Most of the enduring and healthy relationships are based on four pillars - that of love, trust, commitment and communication.

FOUR PILLARS to Building an Authentic Relationship

Pillar of LOVE

I came across an interesting ongoing research regarding the connection between the heart and the brain and their respective electromagnetic fields. It says,

"In addition to the extensive neural communication network linking the heart with the brain and body, the heart also communicates information to the brain and throughout the body via electromagnetic field interactions. The heart generates the body's most powerful and most extensive rhythmic electromagnetic field. Compared to the electromagnetic field produced by the brain, the electrical component of the heart's field is about 60 times greater in amplitude, and permeates every cell in the body. The magnetic component is approximately 5,000 times stronger than the brain's magnetic field and can be detected several feet away from the body with sensitive magnetometers."

Heart is one of the first organs formed in the body. It is one of the most important organs of our body that helps us to connect with others and with the universe. The language of heart is love. Love is more than an emotion. Love encompasses other feelings like kindness, compassion, empathy, care and patience. When you meet a person, you can feel whether that person is coming from a place of love or from dislike. It is an electromagnetic phenomenon. The electromagnetic waves of the heart of the other person reach your heart even before the person.

A saint and his disciples were visiting the Ganges river, where they found a group of family members on the banks shouting in anger at each other. Turning to his disciples, the saint smiled and asked, 'Why do people in anger shout at each other?'

His disciples thought for a while. One of them finally said, 'Because when we lose our calm, we shout.'

'But, why should you shout when the other person is just next to you?' countered the saint. 'You can just as well tell him what you have to say in a soft manner.' His disciples thought about it some more, but could not come up with a satisfactory answer. Finally the saint explained, "When two people are angry at each other, their hearts distance a lot. To cover that distance they must shout to be able to hear each other. The angrier they are, the stronger they will have to shout to hear each other, in order to cover that great distance."

But what happens when two people fall in love? They don't shout at each other but instead talk very softly because their hearts are very close. The distance between them is either nonexistent or very small. And when they love each other even more, what happens? They do not speak, only whisper and they get even closer to each other in their love. Finally, they even need not whisper, they only need to look at each other and that's all. That is how close two people are when they love each other.

This is the power of love. Love has no language. When you are operating from a space of love, you exhibit compassion, kindness and patience. You care about the other person. Empathy comes very naturally to you. You are able to put yourself in the other person's shoes and understand their perspective instead of being judgemental about them. Operating from a space of love instantly binds you with the other person and lets you function out of freedom rather than fear in any relationship. Just showing that you genuinely care about the other person and being kind towards other fellow beings not only takes you one notch higher in the process of evolution, but also builds up a strong character. It goes a long way in building an ever-lasting bond.

There is an interesting story I read about how a small gesture of kindness and compassion can create a miracle.

This story is about Rob working with a freezer plant. As a normal routine practice at the end of the day, after the siren goes and all employees are out of the plant, the security person in-charge seals the doors and switches off the lights.

On one such day, as the siren went, everyone from the plant packed up to check out. Just at that time, a technical snag developed in the plant and Rob went to check. By the time he finished, it was late. The doors were sealed and the lights were off. Trapped inside the ice plant for the night without air and light, an icy grave was almost sure for him. Hours passed by and he had almost lost hope. He thought only a miracle could possibly save him. As he was sitting there, helpless, he heard a sound of the door opening. To his utter surprise, the security guard entered there with a torch and helped him to come out.

On the way back Rob asked the security guard, "How did you know that I was inside? Did anyone inform you?" The guard said, "No one sir; this unit has about 50 people. But you are the only one who says 'hello' to me in the morning and 'bye' in the evening. You had reported in morning; but did not go out. That made me suspicious, and I came hunting for you."

Rob never thought that a small gesture of greeting someone would prove to be a life saver for him.

Pillar of TRUST

My focus in life has always been on building authentic relationships and I am truly blessed with some wonderful people around me. I strongly believe that trust builds up a solid foundation for any relationship, be it an employer-employee or seller-buyer or husband-wife, friends or any relationship for that matter can stand strong on the foundation of trust. I have experienced that when you trust someone, the onus of not letting that trust break lies on that person.

Once, in the year 2002, my wife was driving me to the airport as I had to go for a ten-day long business tour. Just about 10 km away from the airport, on the highway, my car engine broke down. I tried all the first-aid methods, but in vain. The engine would just not start. I became a little anxious as I was getting late for the flight and at the same time I could not leave my wife with a dead car in the middle of the highway. I looked around in desperation and fortunately saw an automobile garage a few meters away on the service lane. I quickly ran to the garage and briefed the person there about the situation. He came with me and somehow managed to start the car and pull it through up to the garage. After checking, the owner of the garage Rajan told me that the fuel pump needed to be replaced and it would cost approximately Rs. 10,000 and would take a day to repair. Until that incident, my car had always gone to an authorised service centre, even for the smallest of issues. I was sceptical about any road side garage person meddling with my car. But I had no option at that point. I thought for a while and decided to give it a try. I told him, "Rajan, my car has been always serviced by the company service centre. This is the first time I am giving it outside the company. Trust you will do a great job." Saying this I went on my forward journey.

Next day when my wife went to pick up the car and asked for the bill, she was shocked to see the bill of Rs. 600, as the estimate given to us was Rs. 10,000. Rajan explained her, "When I opened the car, I realised that it was just a loose connection that was causing the problem and not the fuel pump. So we did the connection right."

He could have easily duped us as we had no knowledge about cars and moreover, we had agreed to pay Rs.10,000. But he lived up to the trust I showed in him. I was truly moved by his honesty. It's been forteen years now. I changed several cars since then, but Rajan has always been there as an advisor and taking care of our cars.

When you delegate some work to somebody, it is important to trust that person. Either you have complete knowledge about the work or complete trust in the person. It also drives the person to perform better and gives him/her a sense of ownership. Thus the final outcome of the work will speak for itself.

But there are people who say that they have been cheated and they have lost the trust over other person. I agree. It hurts. But remember, it's always the other person's loss. If you are genuine and the other person cheats, he has lost the chance to an authentic relationship.

Pillar of COMMITMENT

A reporter met an elderly couple married for sixty years, and looked madly in love with each other. She asked, "It is not easy to live together for six decades, still love each other the same way and have no fights. What is the secret?" The reply was astounding. They said, "Who says we don't have fights? Like every other couple we too have gone through our share of differences, arguments and quarrels. But we always patched up and started on the same note. You see, we come from an era, when something broke, we repaired it unlike today. You are living in the age of 'use and throw'. We always believed in mending things and relationships".

A divorce lawyer had once attended my workshop. I asked her, "You handle so many divorce cases. What according to you is the main cause for so many divorces happening today?" She said, "Out of all the cases I have handled, I can say, only 5% of the cases come with a genuine issue like abuse, dowry etc, where there is no option left than to divorce. But in 95% of the cases it is the ego and lack of commitment. Nowadays people have become impatient and intolerant. When their expectations are not met, the easy resort for them is parting. Well, they don't understand that that is also not an easy way."

Any kind of personal or business partnership is about commitment and being committed towards that commitment. Every relationship goes through highs and lows, and challenges and rewards. There are times when situation push you to the edge. But even in the roughest patches of life, the only thing that can keep you going is the commitment. In a committed relationship, each person will try to empower the partner and help him/

her achieve their goals. Commitment means you act with integrity, respect and care, even when your emotions are telling you otherwise.

Pillar of COMMUNICATION

You know what is the most important part of communication in a relationship?; It is Listening. Most often when we communicate, we do so with the intention of responding than listening. Many times we only listen to things we want to and form a judgement of what is being said rather than hearing it out. While doing so we often pollute the conversation.

How often have you experienced this? You are feeling low and you call up a friend. Your friend starts advising you even before you complete what you want to say. He/she points out where you went wrong, what you should do and what you shouldn't. Whereas at that moment, you just need someone to listen to you. This completely contaminates the very purpose of communication. You are well aware of your situation and you are the best judge for it. What you need is just a friend, to pour your heart out, as doing this brings clarity in your mind too. Now a days there are professional listeners who provide you a safe and comfortable space to share your worries and frustration without the fear of being judged.

Listening to someone also means giving your 100% to it. Sometimes we feel that we are listening, but our mind is wandering in to the unknown horizons. Either we are engrossed in our own thoughts or we are looking at our mobile phones or watching TV or reading something while we are listening. Actively listening with 100%

attention is the key to good communication. One more powerful way of doing it is through establishing an eye contact while talking.

Open and honest communication is an important part of a healthy relationship.

Respect the other person's point of view. You may not agree to whatever is being said. But that is that person's view and it is close to his heart. Rather than entering in to an argument of what is said is right or wrong, it makes better sense to understand and empathise. This gives you an insight on why the person said what he said and you are able to look at the whole conversation from a different perspective.

In a conversation, it always pays to see 'what' is right rather than 'who' is right. This can happen only when you operate from a space of love and not ego.

Three deterrents to building an authentic relationship

1. Assumption: There is a Chinese proverb which says, "There is 'my truth', there is 'your truth' and there is 'the truth'."

Are you sure that the way you perceive things are the way they really are?

There is an interesting story I heard some time back.

A 24-year-old boy looking out from the train window, shouted, "Dad look the trees are going behind". Dad smiled and patted his son's back. A young couple was sitting on the opposite sit looked at the 24-year-old's childish behaviour with pity. Suddenly he again said "Dad look the clouds are running with us!". The couple couldn't resist and said to the old man, "why don't you take your son to a good doctor?" The old man smiled and said "I did it and we are just coming from the hospital, my son was blind from birth, he just got his eyes today".

We assume things based on our senses and logic. They may not always be true. Assumption is like termite, that slowly eats up a solid relationship. The sad part is that we are quick in assuming things. "He did not answer my call. Probably he is upset with me"; "My boss never appreciates my work. Probably he doesn't like me or I may not be good at work"; "My husband is continuously hooked on to his phone. Probably he has some affair going on." Our mind will have all kinds of thoughts, but we need to be careful not to get weighed down by what our mind is trying to tell us. It always helps to look at a particular situation from different perspectives before forming an opinion about anybody. Depending upon the comfort of the relationship, it is good to discuss about your feeling openly and honestly to know the other side.

2. Expectation: Another dampener on an authentic relationship is expectations. Expectations often lead to disappointments which further lead to misery. Expectations when not fulfilled lead to heartaches. For example, you are hospitalized and you expect your friend to come and see you, but it doesn't happen and you land up with a heart ache. A mother-in-law expects a particular behaviour from a daughter-in-law, and when it is not fulfilled she is labelled as bad.

In a relationship, we often expect our partner to behave in a certain way to do certain things for us. And if your partner cannot live up to the expectations you have setup for him, it becomes a threat to your relationship. However, what we need to understand here is the fact that each of us is an independent being on an independent journey. Our behaviour is influenced by our upbringing, our beliefs and our karmas. Only when we acknowledge this and respect each other's individuality and space, will we stop expecting anything from others and operate from the space of unconditional love. The relationships thus formed will be beautiful.

3. Reaction: In case of a conflict, do you find yourself getting agitated, your pulse racing and you take smallest of issues out of proportion? If that is how it is, then you are a reactive person. I often remember a joke I heard on reaction.

A CEO of a company once visited his factory. A man was standing on the floor, not doing any work and looking aimlessly. Looking at this man standing idle, the CEO asked, "What is your salary?" To which the man replied, "5,000, Sir" The CEO took out his wallet and gave 15,000 and told him, "I pay people here to work and not to waste time. This is your three months salary. Now get out of here and never come back." On this the man left. The CEO later asked the other workers, "Who was this guy?"

The workers replied, "Pizza delivery boy, Sir!"

Being reactive can be very hazardous to your business. Reaction has the power to destroy the relationships.

As soon as you react, your negative emotions get activated. Unable to regulate your response and behaviour, leads to the end of communication and intimacy, thus sabotaging a good relationship. As soon as you become reactive, you are not conscious of what you are saying and you have no consideration for the person you are conversing with. Your communication can easily turn into a war zone, where the concerned people will be hurt and injured. When you are mindful, you are more aware of your behaviour and your reaction. You are aware about other's feelings and how your words may affect the other person.

Happy, healthy and enduring relationships do not develop overnight. They require work and thoughtfulness. They need to be built over a period of time. They need to be nurtured on a regular basis.

In any relationship, personal or professional, there are bound to be highs and lows, but they are momentary. They do not necessarily define the status of your relationship. It is a good idea to built up a relationship account, where you can deposit small efforts on a regular basis. This investment will mature to give you solid returns one day. Small things like staying in touch, being there for others, maintaining the emotional connect can turn a relationship into a source of ongoing support and happiness.

THE WORKSHEET

We always need people around us; to encourage us, appreciate us, support us and love us. We need people around us to share our blues and our happiness, to help us achieve our goals. For this we need to build up some real-time, authentic and sustainable relationships. Take this exercise to know what kind of relationships you have. Be honest about your answers. There is no right or wrong here. By the time you complete the exercise you will have an idea of where you stand, and where you need to go. It will bring clarity in your thoughts and you will know where you need to put in that extra bit of effort. The answers to the questions below should be descriptive and emotionally intense.

Your relationship equations,

with your partner

1. When was the last time, you took time out together?

....

....

2. How often do you express your true feelings towards your partner?

....

....

3. Do you often have fights or disagreements?

....

....

4. Do you share a common interest?

....

....

with children

When was the last time when,

1. you had a friendly chat with your children?

....
....

2. you told them how much you love them?

....
....

3. you asked them what they want to do in their life?

....
....

4. you spent that father-child quality time?

....
....

5. you played with them and became a child yourself again?

....
....

6. you actually put them to sleep telling them a story?

....
....

7. you praised them in front of others?

....
....

8. you told them how proud you feel to be their father?

....
....

9. you gave them a surprise by buying them something they have been demanding since long?

....
....

10. you attended a parents-teachers meet?

....
....

with parents

1. When was the last time when,

a. you ever expressed your feelings towards them (positive and negative)?

....
....

b. you feel that they are wrong in certain things are you able to tell them in a polite way?

....
....

2. Do you share a strong bond with your parents?

....
....

3. What is it that you like most about them?

....
....

4. What is it that you would like to change in them?

....
....

5. Are there any unresolved issues between you and them?

....

....

with outer circle

1. How do you get along with your extended family?

....

....

2. How often you meet them?

....

....

3. Whose company you like the most?

....

....

4. How important you think is your extended family to you?

....

....

with friends

1. How many friends do you have, whom you can call upon at any hour of the day?

....

....

2. What kind of people you get attracted to as friends?

....

....

3. What are the qualities you look for in your friends?

....

....

4. Can you make friends instantly or it takes a long time?

....

....

5. Do you take the initiative in a friendship?

....

....

6. How much are you ready to give in a friendship?

....

....

7. How much of your time(in %) in a week do you spend with your friends?

....

....

with colleagues

1. Do you think your colleagues can be good friends?

....

....

2. Do you have any?

....

....

3. How would you describe your relationship with your colleagues, junior and senior?

....
....

4. Who are the people you think you need to stay away from in the office?

....
....

5. Who are the people you can resonate with in your office?

....
....

6. Do you see yourself competing with your colleagues all the time?

....
....

7. Do you feel hurt if your colleague points out your mistake?

....
....

8. Also if your colleague makes a mistake, how do you tackle it?

....
....

9. Are you frank or diplomatic at work and why?

....
....

10. Do you genuinely wish good for your colleagues?

....

....

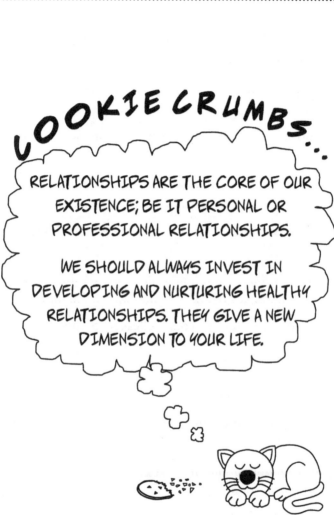

SET TO RISE

6

SET TO RISE

Turn setback into a comeback

We are living in an age where natural jungles are slowly being replaced by the concrete jungles. So, if you ever feel like going for a nature trail or view the sunset or sunrise, or climb the mountains; you may need to plan a vacation far away from where you are living.

Well, I was fortunate in that regard. As a child, I had the privilege of being raised in Gwalior, known as a historic city, surrounded by rocky hills from all sides. The perfect location of the city in the valley between the hills, covered with beautiful landscape, attracted a lot of visitors. Being an ardent nature lover, most of my free time would be spent running through the thick forests and climbing the mountains. I remember crazily riding my bicycle to a hill, parking it under the tree, and running further to the top every evening to get the glimpse of the most incredible sight, the sunset. I would sit there and watch with wonderment as the sun slowly descended down the horizon. I would get soaked in the mesmerizing hues of yellows and oranges. Slowly the bright yellow-orange light would turn dull and the sun would disappear. However, all this would last only for a while. As a child I would question my mom, "why does the sun have to set at all?" and my mom would say, "son, but it does rise again, and marks the beginning of a new day!"

As I grew up I became more aware of the infallible ways of nature. The sun does set, but it rises again as we experience the marvellous phenomenon of the universe.

This made me aware of one of the most beautiful laws of the universe, "Set-to-Rise". Most often, when good things in our life come to an end or we fail at something, we get dejected and lose hope. But nature tells us, 'remember, after every sunset there is a sunrise. And this phenomenon is continuous.' Nature teaches us some important lessons of life which we may not be able to learn in school.

It is very interesting to see how a baby giraffe is born. In fact, the birth of a baby giraffe is quite an earth-shaking event. The baby falls from its mother's womb, some eight feet above the ground. It shrivels up and lies still, too weak to move.

The mother giraffe lovingly lowers her neck to smooch the baby giraffe. And then something unbelievable happens. She lifts her leg and kicks the baby giraffe, sending it flying up in the air and tumbling down on the ground.

As the baby lies curled up, the mother kicks the baby again and again until the baby giraffe, still trembling and tired, pushes its limbs and for the first time learns to stand on its feet.

Happy to see the baby standing on its own feet, the mother giraffe comes over and gives it yet another kick. The baby giraffe falls one more time, but now quickly recovers and stands up. Mama giraffe is delighted. She knows that her baby has learnt an important lesson, "never mind how hard you fall, always remember to pick yourself up and get back on your feet."

Why does the mother giraffe do this? She knows that lions and leopards love giraffe meat. So unless the baby giraffe quickly learns to stand and run with the pack, it will have no chance of survival.

Most often when we face setbacks in life, we tend to give up. We feel that life is over. But what defines us is how we rise after falling. Each failure teaches us to learn, change and grow. Failure in our lives is a temporary setback. It gives us an opportunity to reflect and learn and presents us with some refreshing opportunities. The trick is how soon we pass through this setback and move forward.

There was once an inter-school football tournament. During the half time, a spectator asked a player, "What is the score?" "3-0, they are leading by 3", pat came a reply with a big grin from the boy.

The man was confused, and said, "How can you be so happy, even when your opponent is leading and your team is losing?"

"Why should I be sad sir? The final whistle is not blown yet!"

This is one of the most inspiring stories I have ever heard. Why should we judge ourselves, whether we have succeeded or failed until the final call? Even if we fail, we are crossing that hurdle to move towards our goal. It has made us wiser and stronger. Like Thomas Edison said, "I have not failed. I've just found 10,000 ways that won't work". Failure is nothing but success in progress.

Setbacks in life can demoralize you, make you feel unworthy and even make you lose sight of your goals. But if you take a look back over the course of your life you will realize that many of the biggest problems in your life turn out to be blessings in disguise. Bill Gates was a Harvard University dropout and co-owner of a failed business. Had he let these setbacks take over him, Microsoft would not have been a reality. In spite of a setback in academics and business, he made a comeback with a bang.

Each sunrise in your life ushers in a new opportunity and a hope to succeed. It gives you a chance to come out of a victim zone and confront and stare setback in its face and say, "hey, I am ready to face you. I shall not give you the power to pull me down." By doing this, a process of transformation begins, and you only emerge out to be a wiser and a strong person. Miracles happen, situations change and you are able to pass through the challenges to reach your goal. What you require to do is follow what I call the CPWD principle.

C – Consistency certainly pays off

When you are working towards achieving your goal, some days will be sunny while some will be windy. Some days you may feel inspired while some days you may feel sad. But what will keep you going is the consistency. For instance, if your goal is to lose weight, you will get the result only when you are consistent in your efforts, exercise and diet.

When you focus on the process rather than the end result, you are off the burden of completing the task or reaching your goal. This gives you the freedom from the overwhelming feeling of reaching the potential results. While writing this book, 'SKY is Not the Limit', I gave myself an year's time to complete after the release of my second book 'Many Lives One Soul'. But for the first few months I was simply unable to write anything. Though the concept was in my head, I had great difficulty putting it on paper and nothing was done. I realized that I was too focused on the release of the book after one year than on actually writing the book. As soon as I realized this, I shifted my focus only to writing and writing consistently, without really thinking about the end product. Every day, I wrote something, or read out and edited what I had already written. That did the trick and the book is ready in the speculated period of time.

P - Perseverance is the key

When faced with obstacles or setbacks, it is easy to falter. As the going gets tough, some may even give up. But the key to be successful and be able to reach the goal you have set for yourself, is by persevering through the most insurmountable challenges in life.

Successful people in their respective fields have shown enormous perseverance, in what they did to achieve what they wanted to. Nelson Mandela stayed in prison for 27 years for his fight against the apartheid system. Even while in prison, he kept working and kept his hope against all odds. After years of struggle, Mandela eventually succeeded in bringing about the end of the Apartheid system and in 1994, at the ripe age of 72 became the first democratically elected State President of South Africa.

Mahatma Gandhi showed immense perseverance in gaining independence through non-violence. He never deterred from his path, and with consistent efforts against all the oppositions, he became successful in his mission through sheer perseverance.

Have you ever seen a stream flowing through the rocks? It cuts the rocks and finds its way. The stream is not stronger than the rocks, but the perseverance does the magic.

W - Wait & Watch

In this modern age, on one hand we go gallivanting around the space, while on the other we have forgotten to be patient. Smallest of things such as traffic jams, no wi-fi or mobile signal, a baby crying or domestic help on leave, have the potential to make us anxious and irritable. We may become frustrated, and loose the sight of our goal. We may feel victimized and indulge in a self defeating behaviour.

When you plant a mango seed, it goes through its own process and takes its own time to yield the final fruit i.e. a mango. You have to be patient, before you can actually eat the fruit. In today's age of fast food world, we want instant results for whatever we do. Sometimes after doing the needful and putting in the best efforts we need to just wait and watch. Have faith in the process, in ourselves and in the universe. Patience and faith are important virtues to be successful. These two virtues are vital when you face series of setbacks. Patiently going through the challenging situations without really getting perturbed and moving towards your goal with faith, will take you to your dream destination.

D – Dream, never stop dreaming

When you encounter failure, it is very easy to give up on your dreams.

But Walt Disney kept his dreams alive and the burning desire to achieve those, despite the terrible times he went through. Walt Disney was considered an utter failure when he was fired by the editor in 1919 from his job at the Kansas City Star paper because he "lacked imagination and had no good ideas". His first attempt at business landed in bankruptcy when he acquired an animation studio by the name of Laugh-O-Gram. The company was acquired because, at the time, Disney's cartoon creations had gained popularity in the Kansas City area. But, when he hired salaried employees, he was unable to manage money and the business wound up heavily in debt. Subsequently, he filed for bankruptcy and moved to Hollywood, California.

However these failures did not dissuade him and he kept moving and kept dreaming. And then emerged the iconic cartoon character 'The Mickey Mouse' and the Walt Disney company, which revolutionized the animation industry. Micky Mouse and other characters soon became household name in the entire world. Walt Disney not only dreamt big but motivated others to do so as well.

Michael Jordan once said, "Obstacles don't have to stop you. If you run into a wall, don't turn around and give up. Figure out how to climb it, go through it, or work around it." The word 'impossible' does not find a place in the dictionary of successful people. For them every goal is achievable. What is needed is a dream; consistency, perseverance and patience to follow the dream and faith in the universe with a 'never say quits' attitude.

Our setbacks and failures don't determine our lives, what they do is reveal our true self; how resilient and strong we are. Do we become a victim to the circumstances or do we fight them and transcend. It is we who stop ourselves from achieving what we want to achieve.

Goals, Achievements and Success

What is success? Well, the definition differs from person to person. Some people feel they are successful when they amass material possessions, some people relate success to their career achievements, while some may define success as achievement of their goals and fulfilment of their dreams. I believe success is a very subjective term and cannot have a specific definition. However, I strongly believe that feeling of happiness and a sense of satisfaction are the two most important ingredients of success. According to me, if you have achieved your set goals and at the same time you are happy and satisfied in life, without any fear, insecurity and lack; then you are truly successful. The achievement could be big or small. Not everybody needs to climb Mount Everest to get a sense of achievement. It could be as small as taking a project to completion or as noble as saving somebody's life.

The problem occurs, when you get caught in a trap of comparison; when you start rating your worth and success in comparison with others. "'He has a BMW and I don't, this means that he is more successful than I am." If your parameters for success are related to others, you are sure to land up in misery. Because if you buy a BMW and that person buys a Roll-Royce, you will still not be happy. The point I am trying to make here is that it is important to have aspirations and goals, as that acts as a fuel to the engine of life, but it is not wise to compare with others and base your level of success, happiness and satisfaction on that. Always look at where you were and where you have reached. That will be a real scale for your success. Always remember, each one of us is on an individual journey.

There are two friends I know of, Sid and Karan. Both are engineers with an additional qualification of a MBA, and got selected in multinational companies through campus for similar positions. While Karan lives in a plush three bed apartment in an upscale locality in Mumbai, owns a high end car, goes for a foreign holiday once a year with family; Sid on the other hand is still struggling, living in a one bed apartment in suburbs, driving a small car and has to think twice before planning any holiday. Sid was looking depressed when I met him last. He started believing that he is a loser in life. The reason was, a constant comparison with his friend.

The truth however is, Karan was fortunate to get everything on a platter as he belonged to a family with a sound financial background. Whereas Sid had to repay the loan he had taken for his own education, had to support his parents in building a house in their native place, spend money for his own wedding and sponsor his sister's and brother's wedding too. Only after fulfilling all his responsibilities could he think about his life.

I told Sid, "In my opinion, you are as successful as your friend. Just look at your own life, and see the road you have travelled. You have not only fulfilled your responsibilities but also added value and raised the living standards of other family members as well. It is a huge achievement in itself. Trust me, you have a great future ahead." Sid seemed to be quite pleased with this validation.

You are unique and the best judge for your own situation. Engage in to a healthy competition and that too with your own self. When you are unwavered despite all challenges, with hopes and dreams for future and exhibit a zest and strength to achieve those, you are truly successful.

As per this law "Set to Rise", if you fail in life, be assured that you will rise. Similarly, if you let your ego, fears, guilt, frustration "Set"; something more beautiful is surely going to "Rise" in their place; much more amazing, miraculous and wonderful, that will take your life to a new dimension.

THE WORKSHEET

The following exercise will help you peep into yourself and know yourself better. It will give you an insight into how you respond to a setback in life and help you turn it into comeback. So please be brutally honest with your answers.

1. Have you set certain goals for yourself? List them.

....
....
....
....
....

2. How do you react in case of setbacks and failures on the way to achieving your goals?

....
....
....
....
....

3. Do you get scared, discouraged and disappointed and give up or do you treat is as a stepping stone to success?

....
....
....
....
....

4. Do you try to search for a hidden lesson in case of a setback? Write one such incident.

....
....
....
....
....

5. How do you rate yourself on the scale of 1 to 10, 10 being higher in the following with an explanation of why you think so.

a. Consistency

....
....
....

b. Perseverance

....
....
....

c. Patience

....
....
....

d. Faith

....
....
....

6. Do you believe in your dreams and why?

....
....
....
....
....

7. Do you believe that the universe will help you achieve your dreams? Write an example.

....
....
....
....
....

8. Do you believe in miracles? Write one such miracle in your life.

....
....
....
....
....

9. Write down about one setback in your life and how you turned that in an achievement?

....
....
....
....
....

10. Write one of your success stories.

....

....

....

....

....

COOKIE CRUMBS...

WHEN YOU FALL, BE SURE THAT YOU ARE GOING TO RISE.

WHEN YOU HIT THE ROCK BOTTOM IN LIFE, THE ONLY WAY OUT IS TO GO UP.

THE EXTENT OF YOUR SUCCESS LIES IN HOW QUICKLY YOU GET UP AND GET GOING.

BREAKING
BARRIERS

7

BREAKING BARRIERS

If you believe you can achieve

Since times immemorial, we have been told, that we are small, insignificant, powerless and victims of circumstances. We are like speck of dust or a bubble and we cannot change anything around us. We have grown with this conditioning and this belief has been a major contributor to what we are today.

However, this belief came crashing down with the advent of quantum physics and it's fantastic discoveries. It says that we are a part of what we observe. That means if we are observing a particular thing or a process, we are not only observing it but also participating in it, through our thoughts, emotions and beliefs; and hence become a part of it. Since we are a part of the things we observe, we also have the power to change it.

The biggest discovery of our times is, "there is no empty space in the universe." What we see or may not see (at cellular level) as empty space, is filled with energy as per quantum physics. It has also been scientifically proven that this energy field around us is greatly affected by our thoughts, emotions and beliefs.

If each one of us is surrounded by this energy field, it also implies that we all share the same energy field. Hence our thoughts, emotions and beliefs will not only influence our energy field but of also those around us. This also ushers the responsibility of our lives on our own selves. Thus, to bring a shift in our relationships, career, finance or health we need to bring a shift in our thoughts, emotions and beliefs.

A few days before one of my workshops, I got a call from a lady who wished to attend the workshop with her young daughter Kareena. However, she requested for a meeting before that.

When they came to my office, the lady was very anxious and the daughter looked depressed. After settling down, the lady started narrating her problems while her daughter was continuously staring at the floor. She described several of her health issues like back pains, shoulder pain, difficulty in breathing and so on. Then came the real problem, "My daughter is 28-year-old and yet single. All the guys have been rejecting her till now, mainly because she is not working...!"

That was the first time Kareena looked at me for a second and again started staring at the floor.

"So Kareena, tell me what do you do?" I asked her.

"She has done her MBA, but doesn't want to work", pat came the reply in utter desperation, from the mother. I signaled her to let the daughter answer. I repeated my question.

Kareena finally looked up but could not meet my eyes, as if she was proven guilty of some grave sin. I could notice her beautiful nut brown eyes surrounded by dark black circles. The dreams she must have so lovingly nurtured all her life, seemed to be fading away. Overall, she radiated a feeling of hopelessness and frustration.

"I did my Management, but I am not working and all the guys have been rejecting me." She replied in one breath. What shook me, was a barrage of emotions that accompanied every single word. Her eyes were filled with tears, but probably she had mastered the art of evaporating them in the heat of her pent up anger.

Kareena had formed an opinion about herself, "I am not good enough" because a few guys rejected her. She was gifted with a melodious voice, she loved dancing and she did well in her academic career too. But all that was completely wiped off because of the rejection from some unknown guys, largely shaking her confidence levels.

Here is a beautiful parable I read some time back which illustrates the point further.

A nightingale was sitting on a tree, singing a beautiful song. An ugly old crow, who sat besides her said, "What an ugly song! Listen to my song now."

The crow proceeded to screech and shriek and make horrible noises. And said, "See? I'm the best singer in the forest!"

The nightingale politely disagreed. "No, I'm the best singer in the forest and everyone tells me so." This gave rise to a debate between them.

Finally, the crow said, "I got an idea. Can you see those pigs there?" The nightingale looked down from her branch and saw several pigs wallowing in the mud below.

The crow said, "Let them decide our singing capability. Each of us will sing for them, and they can choose who has the most beautiful voice. The pigs will eat the loser."

The nightingale agreed. They flew down and asked the pigs if they'd judge the contest, and the pigs consented. The nightingale cleared her tiny throat and began to sing the loveliest song she'd ever sung. As she whistled her glorious tune, the forest grew quiet, and even the flowers and trees seemed to be listening.

Next was the crow's turn. He puffed out his chest and proceeded to shriek and squawk and squeal out his ugly song. Mice scampered away, and rabbits dove into their burrows to escape the sound. With each horrible screeching note, the nightingale became more confident of her victory. But when the song was over, the pigs declared the crow as the winner.

As they began eating the nightingale, the crow saw a little tear in nightingale's eye.

"Why are you crying?" the crow asked. "Is it because you're dying?"

"I'm not crying because I'm dying," answered the nightingale. "I'm crying because I allowed myself to be judged by pigs."

We get affected by other people's opinion about us thereby forming an opinion about ourselves, "I am not good enough", based on what others think. We stop believing in our abilities and ourselves, and seek validation from others. These opinions that we form about ourselves get transformed into beliefs in no time and go a long way in messing up with our lives. Here is some food for thought, "If we don't approve of ourselves, if we don't accept of ourselves as we are, how is the world going to accept and approve of us?"

Saying that the beliefs thus formed govern our life, is not an exaggeration. They completely define the person we are today and situations around us. They rule every area of our life, be it health, relationships, career or finance.

My friend Kirti and Ajay are happily married and are blessed with an adorable son who is now three. On a conversation we had over dinner the other day, we got talking over relationships. The discussion took a turn towards how they met each other and tied a knot. While Ajay is a bit quiet and introvert, Kirti is very expressive and naive and comes from a very happy space. The joy she radiates is infectious. Both are poles apart but they share a beautiful chemistry.

"Our's was an arranged marriage as most of the Indian weddings." Kirti said, with a smile on her face.

"In fact, Ajay was not ready for marriage, but his parents literally forced him. They had seen me during one of the weddings in our community and thought that I would make a perfect wife for Ajay." Kirti said with a chuckle.

"Why weren't you ready for the marriage Ajay?" I asked instantly, soon realizing my intrusion in his private space, I said, "Sorry for asking such a personal question Ajay. It is okay even if you don't want to share."

"No no Santosh, it's perfectly fine." Ajay seemed to be quite open unlike our previous meetings. "Actually, I was in a relationship, which did not work out. This broke my heart, and I formed an opinion that relationships are meant to be broken."

This got us talking on a more comfortable level. Unfortunately, Ajay came from a family where his parents did not share a great relationship, though they were still together. Having seen that since childhood and having gone through one broken relationship himself, left a sour taste in Ajay's heart about relationships.

"When Ajay came to visit us on his parent's insistence, he asked me only one question, 'we are complete strangers. On what basis would you decide to spend rest of your life with me?'" Kirti said.

"So what was your answer?" I could not hide my curiosity.

"Well, I looked at my parents and said, if they can be happy together for so many years, I am sure we can!" Kirti said.

"Yeah, I didn't expect this reply from her. But I must admit that she completely bowled me over." Said Ajay gently kissing his wife's hand.

"Wow!" that was all I could say. I was amazed at how one positive belief can have such a deep impact on a relationship. Kirti's firm belief that "Relationships are beautiful" not only worked wonders for the two of them but also for the entire family.

What is a Belief...?

It is accepting with all surety what we see, experience and know. Belief is something we feel very strongly about. In a particular situation, every person witnessing it may have different beliefs about the same situation. It may be influenced by his/her own experiences, thoughts, feelings and emotions.

We get thousands of thoughts every day; thoughts about ourselves, about people around us and about our surroundings. They just come and go. Thoughts are benign in nature. They are just plain simple statements in the form of thoughts. What gives them energy is our emotions!

Our emotions can be broadly classified into two types - 'Love based emotions' which we call as positive emotions and 'Fear based emotions' which we call as negative emotions. Depending upon the type of emotions we experience and attach it to our passing thoughts, we generate our feelings. If the emotions are Love based, we feel joyful, happy, motivated, inspired, etc. But if the emotions are Fear based, we feel angry, hurt, depressed, scared, insecure and so on.

The belief germinates from this feeling. More intense the feeling, more deep rooted will be the belief. This belief, if not addressed over time, grows stronger and later interferes in our life, the decisions we make and subsequently our future.

For example, one fine morning I get an SMS alert from my bank. I happily open my inbox and read it. It says that the current balance in my savings account is Rs 1,000/-.

So my thought is, "Oh...the balance is only Rs1,000/- and I have to yet pay all the bills." As long as it is a plain simple thought it is fine. It is powerless. But at this point the emotion gets triggered.

If it is a fear based emotion, it will press the panic button. "OMG, how will I pay my bills with only Rs. 1,000 in my account? I don't know what is going to happen to me in future?" Now the negative emotion gets attached to this otherwise powerless thought. Soon as this happens, the thought gains strength and a feeling is generated. I start feeling insecure and worried about my future. At this time a belief is born. It could be, "I can never get rich." or "I always have to work hard to make both ends meet." And if a similar situation repeats itself in future the belief becomes stronger.

Now let's look at the other side of the coin in the same situation. If the emotion attached to the thought is love based, my reaction to the situation will be, "Never mind. I have faith that I will be provided as and when required." This will give a positive direction to the thought and a feeling of contentment and peace will be generated. The belief thus formed will be "there is abundance for everyone in the universe" or "whatever I need will be provided to me."

To say that 'these beliefs influence our life' would be an understatement. They actually rule our life! Our mind is incredibly powerful. It is a thought producing factory, working overtime. Whereas our heart is the Centre for emotions. Hence mind and heart in unison can either make us or break us. They are the decision makers of what, where and who we are today.

Is it possible to change our beliefs? Yes, certainly. Simply by changing our thoughts and emotions.

My friend Manasi was going through a tough phase in her life. She was out of a bad relationship and had lost her job at the same time. She got sucked in the negative emotional spiral. Her self-esteem went down and she started believing that she doesn't deserve good in life. One of her friends suggested, that she visit an Astrologer. After this visit, Manasi looked quite positive. The Astrologer told her that her current situation was because of some planetary positions and if she visited and prayed at one particular temple twice a week, she will be soon out of it.

Manasi religiously followed what was told to her and as predicted she got another job very soon. I am not an expert to comment on the astrological part of the whole situation, but with great certainty I can say that going to the temple and praying instilled a positive belief in her. She sent a very strong signal to the universe about the job she desired and she was confident that she would get it, and she manifested the same.

Our mind is unbelievably powerful and our heart supplies fuel to our mind to set it in action. More over there is a strong connection between our mind and body. If we have negative feelings about us and things around us, be it our relationship, our finances or our health, corresponding chemicals or hormones are released in our blood stream and this starts affecting our physical organs in the body.

There is an interesting research done on the 'placebo effect'. A placebo is a substance or other kind of treatment that is a look-alike of real treatment. When the doctors feel that the symptoms are more psychological that real, a sugar pill that looks exactly like the medicine, works wonders. It relieves the person of the symptoms and many times also the resultant effects as well. How does this happen? This research on placebo effect has established a strong

connection between the mind and the body. When the person eats the sugar pill thinking that it is the medicine, his mind tells his body, "You will feel better since you have eaten the medicine" and activates body's natural defense mechanism. Thus the person gets healed.

Making a Turnaround in Life by Overcoming Limiting Beliefs

Before I wrote my first book KEYS, I had a strong belief and I affirmed it several times, "Writing is not my cup of tea. It is a job of those who are studious, academically inclined people" and I never belonged to that category. But at the same time I wanted to share all my experiences and insights I had gained on this journey so that more and more people could benefit. A book seemed to be the most appropriate medium to do so. The first step I took towards this was to stop the negative commentary. I changed it to, "Let me give it a try" to, "I think I can do it" to, "I am sure I can do it." The first draft of the book was pathetic. I worked on it a few times and refined it. Then I requested a couple of my friends from the editorial background to polish it for me. They obliged and finally what came out was an outstanding product. And my first book became a bestseller. The limiting belief of many years came crashing down and now I am writing my third book.

When we swirl a spoon to mix sugar in a glass of milk, a whirlpool is formed and it continues to become stronger with every stir. However, if we swirl the spoon just once in the opposite direction the whole whirlpool falls apart. Similarly, in life if we are caught in a spiral of negative beliefs, then introducing just one positive belief will turn around the whole situation.

Well, it is easier said than done. The beliefs that we form get stored in our subconscious mind and they keep on influencing us in every way in our day to day activities. They also stop us from achieving our dreams. Though consciously we may have certain goals, but we may hold ourselves back due to fear. We may simply procrastinate. We may think that we are not worthy of some new accomplishments. Or we may even make avoidable mistakes that sabotage our progress. The resistance to take a step forward comes from our subconscious mind.

Following are the steps to uproot your negative limiting beliefs and empower yourself with new positive ones.

STEP 1 : Identify the limiting beliefs

The first step to solving any problem is identifying the problem. List out all the goals you wanted to achieve in life. Go through each item in the list and think why you were not able to achieve it till now. If you give this a deeper thought, you will come up with a list of the limiting beliefs that are playing a role in your life. These are nothing but false statements you have been telling yourselves since long enough. These beliefs could be,

I am not good enough

I don't deserve it

I have to work hard for money

I am not as fortunate as my friend

I am too old and it is too late to start anything

140

These beliefs are formed from your own experiences, or from what other people have told you.

But once you have identified the belief that is standing between you and your goal, the other steps become easy.

STEP 2 : Counter your belief

Look for one instance that defied your belief; something that you did or experienced that is not in alignment with your belief. Doing this will give you the possibility to see the flaw in your limiting beliefs.

For example, if you have a belief, "I am not good looking", try to remember an instance when somebody complimented you on your looks.

STEP 3 : Challenge your belief

Remember the instances when the belief that you have has worked against you from the past. Remember that incidence when your belief that held you back from taking a step towards achieving something.

For example, your belief is, "I don't deserve it". Say you are working in an organization since a long time, and you have given your best to your organization. Happy with your dedication and loyalty, your boss recommends your name for a overseas posting. You are happy as your dream is coming to fruition; but this happiness doesn't last for long. Your belief "I don't deserve this" peeps out of your subconscious mind, putting all the fears and doubts about the new country and the new profile. Finally you succumb to this belief and decide against taking the opportunity.

A few years later when you see your colleagues ahead of you on the career path, you get depressed.

Remember one such instance when you missed the bus because of your belief. Experience the pain it caused and pledge not to miss any opportunity that deters you from your goal.

STEP 4 : Find the source

It is important to reach to the source of the issue to resolve it. Where has this belief come from? Dig deep into the memories of the past, of early childhood, teenage years, or even recently.

For example, I had a belief that "I cannot write". When I tried to reach to the source of that belief I reached a memory when I was in the 4th grade. We had given an assignment to write an essay on 'Our National Bird'. While others in the class got busy writing, I started drawing a Peacock and colouring it, as drawing was my passion and I simply enjoyed doing it. When the time was over, Our class teacher collected all our notebooks. When she saw a drawing on my notebook instead of an essay, she got very angry and showed to the entire class and said, "see this boy does not know to write!" I was embarrassed and belief that "I cannot write" got rooted in my subconscious.

It is important to understand that the external event only acts as a trigger for the formation of the belief most of the times. Just because someone says something does not mean that it is true. It is about the perspective we choose and the opinion we form, out of all the various options available to us. We always have a choice and nothing can have power on us unless we allow it to. In the above example a different perspective could have been; the teacher was in a foul mood, or I didn't feel like writing or the visual came in front of me and I just wanted to draw it. All these perspectives nowhere show that I cannot write.

STEP 5 : Eliminate the limiting belief

This is the most important and the most difficult step in the process. When a belief is formed, we start identifying ourselves with the belief. We feed it, nurture it, and get attached to it. It is not easy to eliminate the part of ourselves that we are strongly connected to. However, to succeed in life it is of utmost importance.

One method that I teach in my workshops is the HAT (Hologram Affirmation Technique) technique. It goes like this.

Revisit the memory that is also the source of your negative limiting belief.

Re-live it and give it a shape and colour.

Now re-write the script of that scene using other possible perspectives.

Give it a fresh colour and shape and a New Empowering Belief in the form of a positive statement. In my case the final statement was, "My writing has the power to transform many lives. I see my book become a bestseller reaching every person who needs it"

Remember, if we create something we also have the power to modify it.

WORKSHEET

Answer the following questions and observe and acknowledge the shift that it brings in your life.

1. Are you happy with the current situation in your life in the following areas?

Relationship

....

Health

....

Wealth

....

Career

....

Personal Goals

....

Social life

....

2. Where do you want to reach in the following areas of your life?

Relationship

....

Health

....

Wealth

....

Career

....

Personal Goals

....

Social life

....

3. List out the things that stopped you from reaching where you wanted to?

....
....
....
....

4. Do you see any underlying beliefs that prevented you from achieving your goals? List them.

....
....
....
....

5. Write down one limiting belief associated with your goal that you wish to address right now.(you can do this exercise for other beliefs one by one)

....
....
....
....

6. Write down all the instances since your childhood that
   proved this belief wrong.

....
....
....
....

7. Write down the instances that stopped you from
   achieving your goal related to this belief and the pain
   you feel because of those.

....
....
....
....

8. Try to reach to the source of that belief step by step
   as explained earlier in this chapter, using HOPE
   technique. Make notes of the same.

....
....
....
....

9. This belief will be in the form of positive affirmation. Write it down.

....
....
....
....

10. Repeat this statement. Write it several times. Play it in your mind as many number of times as you can, until it substitutes the old one. Do it at least for 21 days or until you feel that you have changed replaced the limiting belief.

One idea is to make a 'Belief Board' and put the new positive belief as shown below. This page can be inserted in a readymade frame. And can be changed when its purpose is achieved.

My Goal

I .... the undersigned on ....
day of ....month of .... hereby affirm
the following with complete belief

"I deserve the best and I accept it now"

This new belief is helping me achieve my goal.

....
Signature
& Date here

Your picture here

---

11. Write down when you achieve the goal and how happy you feel of having done the same.

....

....

....

....

COOKIE CRUMBS...

WE ARE WHAT WE BELIEVE AND WE HAVE THE POWER TO DO SO.

IT IS OUR RESPONSIBILITY THAT WE ONLY THINK POSITIVE THOUGHTS THAT WILL TAKE US AND PEOPLE AROUND US TO GREATER HEIGHTS.

DREAM IT, TO GET IT

8

DREAM IT, TO GET IT

The power of creative visualization

During my SKY workshops, there is session on how to break the obstinate negative belief pattern and set on the path to achieve your dreams. Once the negative belief patterns are replaced by positive ones, and are further coupled with the power of visualization, there is no limit to what you can achieve in life.

Vishwajeet, one of my workshop participants shared a beautiful example of how incredibly the power of visualization can turn a dream into reality. All the participants were speechless when Vishwajeet narrated his story. Vishwajeet was leading the excavation team that works on site during the construction of high rise buildings.

In Vishwajeet's own words, "There was a time when I lived hand to mouth. That time I was working on an excavation site opposite a tower, which was constructed by the same builder. It was a twenty-seven storied building and there was an amazingly beautiful penthouse on the top, which seemed to be almost touching the skies. It was a fascinating five bed room luxurious duplex with sprawling terraces and a sea view. The builder had retained it for himself, with no intention of selling it."

"Everyday when I went to work, I would look at the pent house and think, 'How I wish I owned it!' Initially a part of my mind would ridicule me, 'A person living in a one room kitchen dreaming of a five-bedroom penthouse? Forget it!' Slowly as my desire to own that penthouse grew, I felt empowered. 'Why not?' a voice within me said. And from that day, I started to visualize that I own that property and mentally lived in it. I was very happy even virtually living in it. I had no money to buy the property, but I did not stop dreaming about it. As we were nearing to the completion of the job, the builder expressed his inability to pay my final dues. Instead he offered to compensate me by offering the pent house at a dirt-cheap price" said Vishwajeet.

A miracle happens when you believe. We call it a miracle but it is actually the creative visualization which is at work. As Paulo Coelho says in his famous book Alchemist, "when you want something, all the universe conspires in helping you to achieve it. It's the possibility of having a dream come true that makes life interesting."

When we visualize about something we are looking for in our lives, with all positive energy, we invite favourable situations and people to make it happen. All top performers irrespective of their profession, harness the power of creative visualization.

Creative visualization is an art of creating pictures in your mind of something you would like to happen in the future.

It is not a special skill; in fact we all are using it daily. We just need to be aware of it and use it consciously to get better results. Whatever happens in our life first happens in our mind. What we need to be able to do is to visualize positive events and outcomes.

At age 16, Einstein used visualization when he discovered that the speed of light was always constant. Einstein believed that visual understanding was the most important form of education and more important than knowledge. He said, "I am enough of an artist to draw freely upon my imagination. Imagination is more important than knowledge. Knowledge is limited. Imagination circles the world." Isn't it amazing that the greatest discoveries in the world are a result of the power of creative visualization?

Our thoughts, when they are focused, and are backed by strong emotions and deep beliefs, can make impossible things possible. Visualization is a tool which gives that power to our thoughts and acts as a catalyst to manifest our desires.

On March 10, 1981, Morris Goodman was flying a single-engine Cessna 172 around Chesapeake Bay, USA. He was one of the top-most life insurance agents in the world, having achieved success at a young age of thirty-five. Morris lived in a 5,000-square-foot home in Virginia Beach city. He had purchased the Cessna just the day before.

As Goodman prepared to land, the setting sun reflected off the water. "It looked like a million diamonds just for me," he recalls. "I was at peace with the world." But his engine suddenly lost power during the runway approach, and Goodman saw power lines directly in front of his windshield. The plane ripped through the high-voltage cables and flipped as it crashed in a field.

After about twenty minutes, Goodman was taken to the hospital, admitted in the emergency room. By then he had a broken neck, crushed spinal cord, jaw and larynx. The nerves in his diaphragm were so badly damaged that he couldn't breathe. A tracheotomy was performed, and he was connected to a respirator. His bowels, bladder and kidneys were not functioning. He was unable to swallow. His condition was so devastating that the doctors told him that he would be a vegetable through the rest of his life. What he could do was merely blink his eyes. Many people in his condition would have just surrendered to fate. But Goodman was a fighter. With the help of alphabets and blinking his eyes, he told the nurse that he would walk out of the hospital on the Christmas day. No one believed that he could make it.

Lying motionless on the hospital bed all Goodman did was to visualize how he would be walking out of the hospital on his own two feet. He vividly imagined the details of how he would walk and the shocked faces of the people in the hospital, medical practitioners and patients alike.

One day, he felt the sudden urge to breathe on his own. With all his might, he inhaled deeply. From then on, his progress amazed the people who knew his story. His full recovery was splashed on every tabloid and newspaper in town. He was nick-named as the 'Miracle Man'.

Today, he is a most sought-after motivational speaker who travels around the world sharing his success story. His favourite saying, "Man becomes what he thinks about", inspires people to think for themselves.

Visualization works because our mind can't tell the difference between a visualization and an actual event. And since the mind controls the body, it causes a similar physiological reaction to imaginary experiences as to real experiences.

Australian Psychologist Alan Richardson conducted an experiment. He took a group of basketball players, divided them in three groups and tested each player's ability to make free throws.

- The first group would practice 20 minutes every day.

- The second would only visualize themselves making free throws, but no real practice was allowed.

- The third one would not practice or visualize.

The results were astounding. There was significant improvement in the group that only visualized they were almost as good as the ones who actually practiced.

In his paper on the experiment, published in Research Quarterly, Richardson wrote that the most effective visualization occurs when the visualizer feels and sees what he is doing. In other words, the visualizers in the basketball experiment 'felt' the ball in their hands and 'heard' it bounce, in addition to 'seeing' it go through the hoop.

The research using brain imagery says, "visualization works because neurons in our brains, those electrically excitable cells that transmit information, interpret imagery as equivalent to a real-life action. When we visualize an act, the brain generates an impulse that tells our neurons to 'perform' the movement. This creates a new neural pathway - clusters of cells in our brain that work together to create memories or learned behaviours - that primes our body to act in a way consistent to what we imagined. All of this occurs without actually performing the physical activity, yet it achieves a similar result."

Visualization is an amazing tool which can be used to our advantage. We can manifest the life of our dreams by using this incredible power that each one of us holds. This can also be used to achieve small things on a day to day basis. Say, you have an important meeting coming up during the day and you want it to work in your favour. You can make it happen by visualizing this meeting in your mental universe with the desired outcome. Once it occurs in your mental universe, it will manifest in your physical universe as well.

When I quit my corporate career to follow my calling, my life changed 360 degrees. We had to cut down our expenses reasonably as there was no salary. We took fewer, shorter holidays as we had to spend judiciously from the limited resources that we had. My wife had a long cherished dream to go on a long international holiday. But it seemed little distant, with me quitting the job. I am strong proponent of the power of dreaming. I believe that if you have a strong intention and you keep on dreaming about it, it will manifest. I told my wife, "Don't stop dreaming. I am sure we will go on a foreign holiday very soon. Don't ask me how and when. Leave that to the universe."

It so happened that one of our closest friends were in Japan on a company project during that time. During one of their trips to India, they stayed with us. One night when we were chatting over a cup of coffee, the wife said, "Why don't you guys come to Japan, for a vacation?"

Like last few times, just to please her my wife said, "Sure, we will plan."

She didn't seem to be satisfied with the answer and said, "I am dead serious this time. And we are sending you the return tickets to Japan."

Both of us reacted, "What?" in a loud voice. She said, "You heard it right. We are sending you the tickets; you just need to give us your convenient dates." She then explained that their company had allocated certain funds to the employees on foreign deputation, whereby they could invite any of their family members or friends to visit them.

And so, a couple of months later we were in Tokyo, Japan, on a ten day vacation hosted by our dear friends. Nothing less than a dream come true.

Most often when we dream about something we aspire for in life, we start worrying about 'how' and 'when' it will materialize. Due to our age-old beliefs and conditioning, we tend to focus on the negative outcome of an event or situation rather than the positive one. This affects the desired result. Universe says, "You just dream and dream intensely, and leave the 'how' and 'when' to me."

In most cases, when we are trying to focus on a particular goal, we start with positive thoughts, but very soon the negative thoughts start to pop up in our minds. They slowly neutralize the positive thoughts. As we go ahead, there is every chance that impatience, worry, anxiety and doubts start storming the mind. This makes it more difficult to visualize and manifest your goal.

Let's say for example, your goal is to acquire a job in a multi-national company at a senior level post. Initially, you visualize your goal with full enthusiasm and you get into action and apply for jobs in a few companies. However slowly, as time passes, your mind starts playing games. Some thoughts pop out; "Do you really think you deserve this?", "Are you capable of handling that position?", "See, nobody has responded till now; You are dreaming too high."

These thoughts completely sabotage your dreams; and your enthusiasm and positive thoughts get replaced by impatience and worry. Thus, your mind starts focusing more on the negative than the positive. Then you conclude that the power of visualization doesn't work.

The key to achieving your goals through the power of visualization is to dream about it to the minutest detail, and let go. Let the universe take over and do its job. Whenever you think about it, feel happy. Let your dream not get infested by the negative thoughts like worry, anxiety, and impatience. Remember that your job is to only dream about your goals, and take steps on the path that unfolds in front of you.

THE WORKSHEET

What did you dream of as a child? You wanted to become an Astronaut and travel in space or you wanted to become a CEO of a multinational company? You wanted to become a famous actor or you wanted to become a social worker and serve mankind? You wanted to become an athlete and win Olympic gold medal or you dreamt of becoming a singer enthralling a stadium full audience? You wanted to be a billionaire or may be a bestselling author? As a child your thoughts were limitless and so were your possibilities of achieving your dreams. So where did these dreams evaporate? The answer is simple. It just that you grew up. And you were told that as grownups you are supposed to think reasonably. The dreams that were close to your heart as a child now started to seem absurd. And you simply gave up, sliding on to the path approved by everyone around you. Those childhood dreams seem to be like fairy tales.

I believe, it is never too late to begin. Now is the time. In the place provided below, write down your dreams; they could be your childhood dreams you may still resonate with or your personal and professional goals as of now. Don't hesitate to write it down, even if it may seem impossible to achieve at the outset. For example, you may have an obese body and you dream of having a perfect figure. You may think, "How is it possible to shed 50 kgs?". Don't judge. Just write down.

Take a few deep breaths and begin,

1. ....
....

2. ....
....

3. ....
....

4. ....
....

5. ....
....

It could be more than five. You may write on an additional paper.

Once you are done with it, take one dream or goal at a time and start working on it. Below are the steps that will help you attain your dreams and your highest goals. They could be relating to money, getting a job, being successful in business, having a harmonious relationship, keeping healthy, losing weight, pursuing an art or just about anything.

There are four powerful steps.

Relaxation:

The hectic lifestyle that we live today heavily weighs down upon us physically, emotionally, and mentally. Our mind is on a constant overdrive. We find ourselves stressed out all the time while chasing our goals. And then we wonder, 'why are things not happening in my life as I want them to!'. Stress creates chaos in our minds preventing us to see things in a right perspective. It also gives rise to a lot of negative emotions that create a hindrance in manifesting our dreams. The trick is to just relax, visualize and achieve all your goals.

There are various ways you can relax.

You can listen to soothing music and try to relax every part of your body. Observe your thoughts, don't resist them. When you just become an observer and let the thoughts pass by, a stage will come when there are fewer thoughts and your mind and body is completely relaxed

You can focus on your breath. Feel the breath – its temperature and texture as it goes through your nostrils up to your lungs and back. With every breath in, breathe in all positivity, good health and peace and with every breath out, breathe out all tensions, stresses and worries. Do it for as long as it takes for you to feel relaxed.

Projection

After you are completely relaxed, gently close your eyes. Visualize a white screen in front of your closed eyes. (This screen can be like a projector screen) Now project on this screen, that which you wish to manifest in your life. See it in detail and happening now, as if you have already received what you were looking for in your life and feel ecstatic about it. For example if you wish to get a car, here is how you would do it.

Visualize, the make and model of the car, the colour, the interior and every detail you can think of. To make your visualization more powerful, go and test drive that car. Visualize that you are driving the car, people sitting inside, the roads that you are driving on. Most importantly focus on your feelings. Bring out the emotions.

Once you are fully done, say "So Be It" thrice and open your eyes with a smile.

Manifestation

Repeat this process every day for a period of minimum 21 days and see it manifesting in your life. You can do this one by one for all that you aspire for in life and see your life changing magically.

COOKIE CRUMBS...

WHEN YOU ARE VISUALIZING ABOUT SOMETHING YOU DESIRE FOR IN YOUR LIFE, YOU ARE ALREADY CREATING THAT IN YOUR MENTAL UNIVERSE.

ONCE IT HAPPENS IN YOUR MENTAL UNIVERSE, IT WILL EASILY MANIFEST IN YOUR PHYSICAL UNIVERSE AS WELL.

WHAT MAKES YOUR HEART SING?

9

WHAT MAKES
YOUR HEART SING?

Passion will take you beyond yourselves

Technology has done wonders to our lives making them far more comfortable, like never before. Today our pizzas are delivered at our door step, our favourite dress can be ordered with a single click, our bills can be paid on line through the apps; in fact the whole world is at our fingertips. We earn a good living, fetching us the luxuries and comforts of a good home. We have a good social life and can easily travel around the world. However we are still miserable, unhappy, insecure, lonely and stressed most of the time. We are unhappy because someone else has something more than we do, we are insecure of losing what we already have and we are stressed as we need to guard what we have. Overall we are always on the edge for having to perform optimum to stay in the race.

Here is some food for thought.

In this wild race to achieve the intangible, haven't we lost our true selves? Haven't we started living the way others expect us to live rather than how we want to? Haven't our lives become shallower than before and we, strangers to ourselves?

If we ponder upon these thoughts, it brings us to an important aspect of ourselves. An important question arises, is there something more to life than just work, money, food, travel and luxuries? The answer to this is "Yes, it is the Passion".

Being a life coach, I encounter so many people who are unhappy without a particular reason in their lives. They are blessed with most of the things anyone would aspire for, but still feel a vacuum. Their question is "What do I do with my life?" I tell them, "I cannot tell you what you should do with your life. You know it the best. You just need to dig deep in to yourself to discover that. I can only facilitate the process."

- 'If money was not the criteria, what is it that you would enjoy doing the most?'

- 'What makes your heart sing?'

- 'What makes you jump out of the bed with superfluous energy, out there to impact the world?'

If you are able to find an answer to these questions, you are very close to finding your passion. Remember; as children how you got lost in doing certain things? Probably you ran after the butterflies, or caught bugs and neatly preserved them in an empty match box, or built castles out of sand, or played your favourite sport until you were dead tired, or lost yourself in music or painting. You must have experienced supreme joy, and must have not even questioned once, whether any of these were adding any value or fetching you money. Though all those things may seem silly to your adult mind; those were the most important things to you back then.

Why do the same things that were very close to your heart as a child seem to be stupid and impractical now? Because, as we grow old we start attaching value to everything we do. "Is it worth investing time? Is it of any use to me? Am I going to make money out of this?' If the answers to these questions is 'no', then we just rubbish the thought. However these may be the activities where our passion is hidden. There are lot of things we love to do as children, we have big dreams to impact the world and create a niche for ourselves. Everything seems to be easy and achievable; but as we grow up, most of our dreams are battered, by many factors such as the conditioning, fears, doubts and insecurities.

As a child, I was passionate about drawing and music, and dreamt of performing in front of a huge crowd. I was so obsessed by it, that I would spend most of my time singing and drawing since a very early age. My mum would have to literally lock me up in my room and force me to study. I wanted to do only that all through my life. When I expressed my desire to take up arts after grade 9th and pursue my interests, I was blatantly refused.

My parents thought that it was okay to have arts as a hobby but certainly not as a profession. 'Artists don't make money', they believed.

At that time I was too immature to question their beliefs or in all probability to go against their wishes. And my dream just remained a hobby to be practiced only in free time, which I never got.

I remember once, when I mentioned about starting something on my own after my engineering, my parents were very upset. My dad gave me examples of how people have failed in the past. "There are 1,000 failure stories behind one successful story, that never come to light" my dad said.

I argued with him, "But dad, I can be that success story!"

He said, "We belong to a middle class family and no one in our family has been into business yet. So it is in your best interest to take up a job and lead a happy life!" That was it! There was no further scope for discussion.

Now after about two decades of my working in various companies, I decided to follow my heart. I began a new chapter of my life as Life Coach and a Motivational Speaker. I take workshops and motivate people to reach their peak performance. I believe that every person is unique and is bestowed with some exceptional gift. It could be a talent, or an acumen, or a desire to make difference in the world. Discovering that and incorporating it in your life, can take you to a new dimension. I have integrated my passion for drawing and music in my workshops. I have used all my artistic skills to create the presentations. All my books have cartoon sketches drawn by me. The relaxation mediations during my workshops are music based. Doing this has given me the scope to follow my passion while pursuing my profession.

Passion is the driving force that propels the dormant energy that is lying beneath those layers of our mind which we may not have explored. Passion is something that makes you lose yourself completely in the act that you are doing, and you lose the track of time.

My friend's dad Mr. Chatterjee is 83-year-old. He has 100% blockage in his heart and a pace maker implanted to regularise the heart rhythm, since last twenty years. My friend told me that Mr. Chatterjee had been pursuing his masters in sanskrit for the last two years and now registered himself for a doctorate. He is passionate about learning. After his retirement he enrolled himself in various courses. He learned law, homeopathy and now acquired masters in sanskrit. He regularly attended college with the students of has grand-children's age and even studied hard to attain distinction. This is what true passion is. The best part is that this passion is keeping him hail and hearty.

Each one of us has a passion. And every person will singularly have a different passion. You may be already aware of the things you are passionate about, but probably haven't discovered yet. But when you discover your passion and align it with what you are doing for a living, a beautiful synergy happens, paving a way for highest achievements. After that, work does not remain a job in the confines of time but it becomes your mission. It becomes pleasurable and timeless; you gain some extra power and strength to achieve and accomplish your vision. The marriage between passion and work can be highly rewarding.

Steve Jobs, known as one of the most passionate entrepreneurs in business history, has offered the best definition of passion in one of his public presentations, in March 2011 just before he died. "It is in Apple's DNA that technology alone is not enough, it's technology married with liberal arts, married with the humanities, that yields us the results that make our heart sing," he said. In 2001, just six weeks before the launch of iPod, it had a plastic screen. Suddenly Steve Jobs felt that plastic would scratch too easily and that the screen should be glass. His decision to make the change sent shock waves through the company. The designers, engineers and technicians went crazy redesigning the casing in such a short time. "No other CEO on Earth would have made that call," wrote Time magazine (Oct. 17, 2011).

However, Steve Jobs didn't care about the added cost or how the media would react. His primary focus was on releasing the most perfect product possible!

Signs indicating that you truly need to find and follow your passion

Some people naturally know what makes their heart sing; while others need to struggle to find it. If we are not already following our passion we reach a point in life where we feel, 'we are just adding years to our life and not life to our years'. This 'adding life to years' is your passion. This may come to surface when,

- you get bored easily
- you force yourself to work everyday
- you feel restless
- you feel unfulfilled although you are successful
- you feel some lack or vacuum in your life
- your heart is not into what you are doing

These are the warning signs urging you to find your passion. These signs may give you an entry in to your deeper selves where your passion rests.

So the next question is how to tap into this powerhouse of energy lying dormant inside you and harness it to your business, career and life? Sometimes it happens by accident while at other times you need to really find it out by going deep within yourself.

Finding Your Passion

Know Yourself

Knowing your self is the first step in reaching your goal and finding your passion. "Who are you?", This question baffles a lot of people. We quite underestimate the importance of who we are and what we want from life, and therefore get swayed by life in numerous directions.

So, who are you? You are not only this human body composed of bones, blood vessels and muscles packed in the skin, but you are much more than that. You are also your values, your passion, your strengths, your fears, your emotions, your goals, your dreams; all that together makes that YOU.

Unaware of this fact, most often we are in conflict with ourselves. We show to the world what we are not, and in the process start accepting that as the truth. The real 'me' gets lost somewhere, and a point comes in our life when that genuine search begins. This generally happens when we are face to face with a grave situation, that compels us to dig within ourselves. But why wait for such a situation for an opportunity to shake hands with our own selves?

So let us start by asking ourselves some simple questions,

What is it that motivates me?

What gives me a kick?

Which task gives me immense happiness and satisfaction?

What is it that people appreciate in me?

What is that thing for which I can sacrifice anything?

What is my strong muscle?

The answers to these questions may take you by surprise. The answers could also reveal your passion. You may get motivated by reading, or adventure; you may get a kick by helping people; you may be good at organising things; people may love what you cook; people may be crazy about your singing; dancing or writing; your strong muscle may be to motivate people. This will give you an idea of what you are passionate about. Passion comes out of feeling authentic about your feelings; knowing that you are honouring yourselves and your decisions and not satisfying somebody else. Your passion is as unique as you. Once you know your passion, the next step is incorporating it in your life.

Re-visit your childhood

You will find the seeds of your passion sown in your childhood. Because as a child your mind is free from the clutches of all kinds of duality, right-wrong, good-bad, etc. As a child your dreams are limitless and your thinking is unbounded. Pick up a thread from your childhood and start off today. Re-visit your childhood and ask a few questions,

What did I love to do as a child?

What did people appreciate in me for as a child?

What was my achievement as a child?

What made me feel the happiest?

What was that activity which I kept on doing all the time?

What was I crazy about?

What was my ambition as a child?

Who was your role-model?

There could be one or more answers to these questions. All the answers may not resonate with you now. But you are sure to get a clue, where your heart lies and you have intense positive feelings for. This can lead to finding your true passion. For example, if you wanted to become a doctor as a child but this does not interest you any further. Think of why you wanted to become a doctor in the first place. What exactly attracted or appealed to you. It could be helping people, it could be a life-style, it could be making a difference in somebody's life or it could be healing people. As an adult, pick up what you relate to most and that could be where your passion lies.

Observe what are you drawn to and acknowledge it

Sometimes you may not have a clear vision of what you like to do, but you may be curious about certain things, you may be drawn to a few things which may seem to be frivolous superficially. But if you uncover the layer of curiosity, you might reach something which may be your calling. We may perceive many things that we are drawn to as forbidden thinking that your parents may not approve of it, or you may not be best qualified for it, or you are not equipped with the required knowhow. But according to me all these things are secondary. Most important is to find your passion and acknowledging it. The second step is knowing why you want to do it. This will bring in the clarity on pursuing it How, is just a process which can be worked out.

Your passion may be hidden in your profession

Sam's dad was a garment merchant. He had developed and taken the business to great heights single-handedly. Sam being the only son, was expected to join his dad's business, after his graduation. Sam was a creative person, and excelled at drawing and painting. But his dad never approved of this. He thought it was a sheer waste of time. The very thought of selling the garments over the counter and supplying the same to departmental stores, bored him to death. But he had no choice and had to join his dad's business. He carried his sketch book to the shop and did some sketching and portraits during the free time. A senior sales manger happened to this once and was surprised to see the exquisite drawings. He said to Sam, "Sir your drawings are mind-blowing. Can we not create some such designs for our garments?" This statement was an epiphany for Sam. He later came up with a whole range of exclusive hand-painted garments and exported those to Europe. This became an instant hit. Sam was happy that his talent got recognition and he could pursue his passion and it pleased his dad as it made good profits.

Sometimes you may not even be aware of this, but an external trigger, or someone can introduce you to that authentic passionate self in you.

You may not always be doing what you are passionate about, but there is something in each profession or business that can bring out the authentic you and that contribution can scale up your activity, business or profession.

At my office I had hired somebody to take care of social media, but as we interacted I found that her passion is talking to people and had exceptional organisational capabilities. As soon as I changed her role, the output was remarkable.

Brainstorming helps

If you are stuck and are still not able to figure out what makes your heart sing, brainstorming will help you. Discuss about your life, goals, dreams and aspirations with someone whom you trust, respect and love. You need to be sure that the person is non-judgemental about you, does not ridicule your ideas, and does not thrust his ideas on you. During such brainstorming sessions, some things might reveal, which you may not be even aware of.

If you are not comfortable discussing with anybody here is what you can do.

Sit in a room where no one disturbs you and you can mess around. Take sheets of white paper, some colour pencils, glue, old magazines, laptop with internet and a printer.

Step 1: List down your hobbies or the things that are very close to your heart, one on each paper. For example it could be travelling, talking, writing, arts, helping people etc.

Step 2: Pick up one from the list, say, writing. Write WRITING in bold caps on a separate paper in the centre.

Step 3: Around writing, write various types of writing. For example, it could be fiction writing, romantic writing, non-fiction writing, self-help writing, novels, short stories, articles books, blogs, technical writing, content writing, quotes, political writing, educational writing and so on.

Step 4: Read carefully and reflect on each of these titles and see if something interests you. If yes mark it with a colour pencil. It could be more than one. For example if it is fiction writing, ask yourself, have you written fiction before. If not you must have surely read it.

Step 5: Write the types of fictions around 'Fiction Writing' that you have circled. It could be science fiction or romantic fiction or any other.

Step 6: List down all the books you have read and wish to read in that category around the type you have selected.

Step 7: Write your role-models in this field and how they inspire you.

If you are able to carry out this exercise patiently, without getting bored and it makes your heart sing, then you are close to discovering your passion. Repeat this exercise for the list you've made in the beginning.

When you find your passion, you need to start following it without the ounce of doubt. Your heart will know what is right for you and guide you accordingly. Passion is related to an intense positive feeling about what you are doing. Don't think about whether it will be commercially beneficial or what will be the outcome; doesn't matter if your passion is not your profession. One thing is for sure that pursuing your passion will certainly add 'life to your years'. It will give you a sense of fulfilment and keep you in a blissful zone all the time. It will give you extra energy during challenging situations in life.

THE WORKSHEET

Passion is something that will spring you out of your bed, cheerful and excited ready to perform; it will also keep you going till late. Passion will give you an identity and satisfaction. Even if you don't know your passion, don't worry, it is never too late to begin. Answer the following questions and see where it takes you.

1. In your life till now, what was the happiest moment of your life, when you touched your inner core?

....
....
....
....
....
....
....
....

2. What was the feeling like? Analyze the feeling. Can you get the same feeling in any other activities?

....
....
....
....
....
....
....
....

3. Did you ever feel that if I had billion dollars, I would do only XYZ in my life? What is 'XYZ' for you?

....
....
....
....
....
....
....
....

4. What gives you a sense of fulfilment and satisfaction?

....
....
....
....
....
....
....
....

5. When you are surfing on the net or reading books, what are the topics you are inclined to?

....
....
....
....
....
....
....

6. What would you do when you are feeling happy?

....
....
....
....
....
....
....
....

7. What would you do even if you are not paid for?

....
....
....
....
....
....
....
....

8. Do you find yourself day dreaming and about what?

....
....
....
....
....
....
....
....

9. If you see someone doing something that excites you and you want to do it as well?

....
....
....
....
....
....
....
....

10. Any fears or beliefs that are stopping you from what you love to do?

....
....
....
....
....
....
....
....

COOKIE CRUMBS...

DISCOVERING AND FOLLOWING YOUR PASSION WILL TAKE YOU TO A WHOLE NEW LEVEL IN LIFE.

PASSION IS A TONIC FOR YOUR SOUL. LEARN TO LIVE LIFE PASSIONATELY AND FULLY.

TAPPING
THE POWER
OF YES AND
NOW

10

TAPPING THE POWER OF YES AND NOW

Create magic in your life through affirmations

Research shows that most people complain once a minute during a typical conversation. "It's too hot today or she doesn't know how to talk or my work is just not getting done or I am so unlucky." Even if we may not be actually expressing some such thoughts, we do run them in our minds. And after a while we start believing them to be true and accept them as a part of our lives. Though we may feel good temporarily, it not only causes serious damage to our life, but also prevents us from moving ahead. Slowly these thoughts become our beliefs. Continuous presence of negative thoughts release stress hormones that interfere with our body systems, manifesting into several diseases. Hence we need to be very careful about our thoughts as they become our reality.

What if we find a positive statement that replaces every negative thought we get? It will result into positive beliefs and help us achieve the unachievable. Such positive statements are called "affirmations".

What is an Affirmation?

An affirmation is any short, positive statement or intention in the present tense designed to cure or correct a specific issue in one's life. This statement, when repeated several times, has the power to produces the desired results.

How do affirmations work?

Affirmations work on the sub-conscious mind level. Repeating them, expands the consciousness by creating a positive energy field around us. It crashes our negative belief systems and builds positive belief systems. An affirmation sends a positive message to the universe that we are ready to receive all the good things.

Take for instance, 'Today is the happiest day of my life', repeating this affirmation will enable the subconscious mind to accept and integrate it. You will start feeling happy about yourself and everything around you. Using affirmations every day keeps your heart and mind finely tuned to what you want to create in your life.

Repeating affirmations everyday strengthens your focus on your goal. However, one needs to be very careful while saying the affirmation. If your goal is to reduce weight, it will be wrong to say, "I don't want to put on weight" or "I hate to be fat". Instead you can say, "I have a perfect, healthy and slender body". The affirmation should necessarily be a positive statement without any negative word in it.

How does one repeat affirmations?

Writing down an affirmation repeatedly, saying it aloud throughout the day, and even singing it to the tune of a well-known song like "Twinkle, twinkle little star," are effective ways to keep you focused on the positive.

Our subconscious mind absorbs each and every thought we think and say. The more we repeat it, deeper it gets embedded in our subconscious mind and greater are the chances of it turning into a reality.

Areas of benefits

An affirmation could be about any aspect of life. It could be about your profession or your personal life. Let's look at a few examples:

Personal growth

One of best reasons to say affirmations is to become a better person. Most often the root cause for not being able to move ahead in life is low self-esteem and low levels of confidence. Affirmations can work wonders in this area.

A 26-year-old, who attended one of my workshops, had such low self-esteem that he could not even introduce himself to people. He would avoid saying his name too. He knew he suffered from low self-worth and came with the intent to work on the same, during the workshop. I asked him to do two things. First, say an affirmation, "I love, accept and approve myself as I am." And second, to say this looking at himself in the mirror and with emotions. He told me later that he could say the affirmation with ease, but just could not manage to look at himself in the mirror and say it, although he tried. Then one day he broke down when he tried to do so and after the flood of emotions subsided, he could manage to do it and truly accept himself unconditionally. This completely changed his persona. Such is the power of affirmations.

Some affirmations for personal growth are:

- I love, approve and accept myself as I am
- I am complete in all respects
- I am the best in whatever I do
- I am a positive thinker
- I am a fearless and powerful being
- I completely trust my abilities
- I am evolving and growing every day

Relationships

Some may find it strange, but affirmations are a great way to attract thriving relationships. During a SKY workshop in Delhi, Simon Chauhan (name changed) had shared that all the relationships in his life have been sour. From the beginning, he didn't share a good relationship with his parents. Due to a few misunderstandings, his wife had separated from him. His daughters were upset with him. Even though he tried explaining things to them, they didn't want to listen. Simon was a successful businessman, his personal life was quite unsuccessful.

After hearing everything he had to say, I suggested he should use the affirmation – "All my relationships are full of love, trust and respect". He argued, "But none of these is there in my relationships." So I asked him, "How would you like your relationships to be?" "Of course, full of love, trust and respect", he said. "So say it and believe it." I also asked him to write it down every day and use it while doing the SKY technique. I'm glad to share this example with you because within two months of that workshop, Simon called my office and shared the story of the miracle that took place in his life. His daughters had started talking to him and his relationship with his parents improved greatly. The affirmations during SKY had worked.

Some affirmations for relationships are:

- All my relationships are full of love, trust and respect
- All my relationships are harmonious
- My partner loves and supports me fully
- I accept a happy and fulfilling relationship
- I am surrounded by love all the time
- I am worthy of love
- I am always surrounded by people who love me
- I love myself deeply

Work and Success

People are always looking to find satisfaction in their work. Affirmations work in this department too.

Suresh Suraiya (name changed) had lost his job a couple of times. He was very disappointed with his work life and always kept re-questioning his decisions. I suggested using the affirmation, "My pathway is a series of stepping stones to ever greater success." And Suresh found that it really worked for him. He was offered a job in the automobile industry and is doing good.

Some affirmations for work and success are:

- My pathway is a series of stepping stones to ever greater success
- I am deeply fulfilled by all that I do
- I am always successful in whatever I do
- I am always at the right place at the right time

Prosperity

Several of my workshop participants have said that the affirmation, "I am a magnet for divine prosperity," has worked wonders for them. People have received money from unknown sources at the exact point of their life when they have needed it. This affirmation induces a belief that you will always be provided.

I personally, totally believe in this affirmation. After I quit my job, my big fat salary stopped. Until I got settled in my new profession, I was banking on the savings I had. But universe had different plans for me. The market crashed and I was unable to withdraw any of my savings. But since I firmly believe and affirm that, "I am always provided for", a miracle happened. I got appointed as an advisor with a company in Singapore and was paid a monthly remuneration of the exact amount I needed.

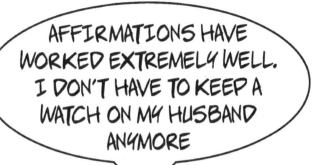

When you affirm and believe, universe will bring you such opportunities you would never imagine in your wildest dreams. One should always operate out of abundance and not out of poverty.

Some affirmations for prosperity are:

- I am a magnet for divine prosperity
- I am always provided for
- Money comes to me easily and effortlessly
- I live in abundance
- I am blessed beyond my fondest dreams
- I am aligned with wealth and abundance
- I am open to receiving the abundance that universe wants to offer

Safety and security

I have realized that this is also a common issue among participants. Fears and issues of security can cause a lot of havoc in a person's daily life. A 25-year-old once told me that his greatest fear is of being ousted from the family business. He felt, he could never make it in the world on his own. This fear was deep rooted. The affirmation that helped him overcome safety and security issues is: I am divinely guided and protected, and I make choices that are beneficial for me.

Some affirmations for safety and security are:

- I am always divinely guided and protected
- I make the choices that are beneficial for me
- I am always safe

Health

There is a strong connection between our mind and body. Whatever our mind thinks has a great impact on our body and subsequently our health. If there is a continuous negative chatter going on in our mind, it will manifest in the form of health issues like aches and pains, diabetes, BP and so on. To stay healthy all the time, the least we can do is say affirmations. Our body has an innate power to heal itself which we often discount. By repeating the affirmations related to health, we can certainly aid this process.

Some affirmations for health are:

- I am healthy, happy and peaceful
- I have a slender and healthy body
- I am in perfect health and I enjoy it
- My whole body is completely healed
- All that I eat and drink keeps me healthy

All the above affirmations are examples for achieving specific things in your life. You can also tailor make your affirmations or find your own personal affirmation.

THE WORKSHEET

Finding Your Personal Affirmation

This is an exercise to find your personal affirmation through finding your 'personal lie'. A personal lie is that one negative belief you have about yourself which you have been denying all through. Through this process once you find out the lie, you can convert it into a positive affirmation. This affirmation if repeated several times, gets embedded into your subconscious mind and thrashes the negative belief.

For eg: If your personal lie is " I am not good enough" The affirmation for the same will be : " I am complete in all respect."

So let's begin.

1.

Write 5 POSITIVE things your mother thinks about you	Write 5 NEGATIVE things your mother thinks about you

2.

Write 5 POSITIVE things your Father thinks about you	Write 5 NEGATIVE things your Father thinks about you

3.

Write 5 POSITIVE things your Spouse/ Best friend thinks about you	Write 5 NEGATIVE things your Spouse/ Best friend thinks about you

4.

Write 5 POSITIVE things you think about yourself	Write 5 NEGATIVE things you think about yourself

5.

Write 5 things you want to achieve in life	Write 5 biggest fears you have in life

Having done this, ignore the positive column. Read through all the things written in the negative side and write in one line what comes to your mind without much logical reasoning.

Now leave everything aside and focus on this line and ask yourself a question why?

For eg: if your line is " I feel very insecure at all times.." Ask the question 'why?' and keep on asking this question until you are left with no further answer. Here you reach your personal lie. Once you arrive at this, you will be able to form a personal affirmation to uproot the personal lie you have been harboring since a long time.

COOKIE CRUMBS...

REPEATING AFFIRMATIONS CONTINUOUSLY IN YOUR MIND OR ALOUD, OR WRITING THEM DOWN SENDS VERY STRONG SIGNALS TO THE UNIVERSE THAT YOU ARE READY TO ACCEPT ALL THE GOOD AND POSITIVE THINGS IN YOUR LIFE.

SKY

THE 12 MINUTE MAGIC

How SKY came into being?

Recent statistics show that stress is the number one lifestyle risk in the world. The rising stress at workplaces, is causing an array of physical issues as well as psychological problems. From high BP, diabetes, pains and aches and insomnia to depression, fears, anxiety, fatigue, lethargy, and many more. In fact each one of us is going through some stress inducing situation or the other.

During my journey of becoming a life coach and a healer, I experienced many techniques that aimed at reducing stress and uplifting the mind, body and soul. However, most of these alternate healing therapies need training that can take from two days to two weeks. Practicing these techniques can also be a time consuming process. Most of them take between 1 to 3 hours. They also need you to follow certain disciplines and rituals.

In today's highly demanding age, it becomes extremely difficult for anyone to find that kind of time; and ultimately one resorts to quick-fix solutions or short-cuts such as popping pills to cure or simply camouflage the outer symptoms. Most of modern medicines or treatments look to cure the symptoms, rather than going to the root cause of the problem. This actually worsens the situation further, as one also has to deal with the side effects of these medicines.

I have met several people who say alternate therapies are too complicated and even time consuming. There must be a short and simpler method, I always wondered. With the mounting stress this generation endures, and the physical, emotional and psychological problems that come along-with, I really wanted something that could take the edge off and not be too complicated or too long. I was on the lookout for an easy healing technique that one can practice anytime, anywhere in a short span of time.

The universe helped, as it always does. During a deep meditation, I had an insight. A technique that is short as well as effective was revealed to me. Slowly, it was also revealed that the technique was to be called 'SKY'.

After that day, I regularly practiced the technique myself. The results I experienced were remarkable. Those 12 minutes were enough to give the same benefits as an hour's meditation. I realized there couldn't have been a better name for this technique. SKY connotes infinite possibilities and that's exactly how I felt about the technique as well. I couldn't wait to share this technique with the world. However, I took time to develop it completely through my experiences and experiments. The grace and guidance of ascended masters was always with me. I worked on the technique for almost three years before taking my first workshop. In the meantime, people around me such as my close friends, immediate family had already started reaping it's benefits.

SKY healing has come up as a short, easy to practice technique, which can be done anywhere, anytime; and one does not require any previous experience or spiritual background to practice it. It is extremely powerful and uses the body's own mechanism to heal oneself.

I always believe that each one of us is unique and exceptionally gifted and born with an immense potential. We are worthy of achieving wonders in life. But we get so bogged down by our daily routine and the conditioning that we go through, that it makes us forget this and we live life ignorantly. People ask me, "how do we recognize the true potential in us?" My answer is you don't have to really make an effort for it; you just need to work on the peeling of the layers covering you, the potential will come out. How do we do this? Simply practice SKY.

SKY comprises of tapping, breathing and visualization.

Tapping

The meridians are points on the surface of the body, which are in constant communication with the outside environment. The technique starts with stimulation and sending impulses through the meridians and central nervous system to the physical body and our major organs, which helps in stimulating blood circulation and lymphatic drainage in addition to balancing hormones and leveling emotions. This helps in calming the body and allowing it to heal naturally.

'Four C' Breathing

Tapping is followed by sets of rhythmic breathing patterns.

The facts about our breath are astonishing. 70% of our metabolic waste is eliminated through breathing; the balance 30% is eliminated through perspiration (19%), urination (8%) and defecation (3%). Our body gets the energy to purify, rid itself of toxins and stresses, and to rejuvenate through our breath. Yet very few of us pay attention to our breath; rather how we breathe. However, correct breathing allows us to access the unlimited amount of energy, which we can use to carry out the repair work within us.

There are certain breathing patterns that result in an automatic unconscious tendency to remain free and clear from our disturbing thought patterns. These also help us being calm and creative, conscious and loving, and naturally flowing even under the most difficult conditions and the most stressful situations. Something very remarkable happens in us when our breathing automatically responds in certain ways to stressful events. This automatic response can be changed when a different breathing pattern than usual is adopted which triggers positive thoughts and emotions. Amazing things happens in us when these new breathing patterns become the habit of our system. We must know that we have a marvelous natural instrument at our disposal - our breathing mechanism. We can use our breathing to free ourselves from physical, emotional, and psychological pain. We can use our breath to prevent the upsetting states of mind and body and to remain, blissful, ecstatic, loving, and creative at all times.

The most important thing to remember in the breathing techniques is to follow the four Cs; i.e. the breathing should be Connected, Cyclic, Continuous, and Conscious.

Visualization

After the breathing pattern comes the visualization. The four 'C' breathing pattern is so powerful that it pulls you into a deep level of trance, and that too within four to five minutes. Such is the impact of the rhythmic breathing patterns when done correctly.

The visualization begins once you reach the deeper level of trance and your mind has attained peace. In this stage, when you visualize anything that you are aspiring for in your life, be it material things, good health or lasting relationships, they manifest.

Thus, SKY- the 12 minute magic, not only helps you to heal yourself on a physical, emotional and mental level but also is a powerful manifestation tool.

Benefits of SKY

By regular practice of SKY healing, one can avail the following benefits.

Emotional and psychological Benefits

Helps relieving stress, fears, insecurities, anxieties

Helps managing anger, depression, low self esteem

Generates optimism and motivation

Boosts confidence and will-power

Improves inter-personal relationships by bringing harmony and joy.

Increases patience

Improves concentration

Brings greater creativity and clarity of mind

Helps in handling challenging situations in a positive way

Physical Benefits

Cures insomnia

Strengthens immune system

Helps in relieving muscle tension

Helps relaxing nervous system

Helps in lowering Blood pressure

Reduces pressure on cardio-vascular system

Maintains the blood sugar levels

Helps in restoring balanced function of digestive system aiding absorption of nutrients

Spiritual Benefits

Helps in the quest of inner transformation and spiritual growth

Helps in rediscovering yourself

Helps in experiencing deeper levels of consciousness

Helps in breaking the layers of conditioning thereby reaching the true self

Helps in experiencing the stillness, bliss and peace of mind

Helps one in living in the moment

When, Where and How of SKY

SKY Healing when practiced and mastered, allows us to create magic in our lives. By practicing this on a regular basis either in the morning, or at any time during the day or night, one can heal oneself, and can remain completely free from negative emotions such as anger, fear, stress, anxiety etc. which are the root cause of our physical diseases. SKY technique can also be practiced twice a day, continuously for twenty-one days for better results. Ideally there should be a gap of at least twenty minutes after or before meals when practicing SKY. This technique also has the ability to take one to deeper levels of consciousness, through which one can experiences inner transformation and spiritual growth.

There is no restriction as to where one can practice SKY. This can be practiced while traveling by road, flying, while waiting in the lounge, or in any place at home or office. The place should preferably be free from noise and pollution. If one is practicing at home, it is better to choose a place and stick to the same place every day, although it is not absolutely necessary. The best place to practice this is in open nature and near green trees. One should avoid practicing SKY while driving or while doing anything which requires one's complete attention.

Miracles of SKY, shared by practitioners

"My work efficiency has increased, tolerance level has gone up, my patience has increased, and reactive nature has decreased to a great extent. I am now at peace with myself."

Aditi Jain, Working Professional

"After doing SKY thoughts have started materialising at a super-fast speed. Everything falls into my lap before I know it. Such is the power."

Kanika Bahl, Entrepreneur

"SKY has power to take care of my energy levels and attract abundance in my life."

Radheshyam Bhura, Businessman

"SKY worked miraculously for my throat infection. The pain and fever both vanished without taking any medicine."

Sridevi Madur, Homemaker

"I could find a definite direction to my life. After becoming a SKY teacher, I also found an extremely effective way to help people from their day to day stresses and in their inner exploration. SKY gives me confidence and inner zest to excel in my life."

Kamal Rathore, PLR Therapist, Certified SKY Teacher

"Before learning SKY, I lacked confidence, was depressed, hopeless and unhappy with my life. Practising SKY daily has helped me gain a positive view towards life. For me, it has paved a path towards confidence, hope and success."

Purvi Rasania, Homemaker

"SKY has taken me closer to realise my inner potential, a great push to look towards all the wonderful opportunities, things, people, situations, that life has to offer me. It gave a purpose to my life."

Chandni Mehta, Entrepreneur, PLR Therapist, Certified SKY Teacher

"SKY has helped me thrash my negative beliefs. With regular practice I have overcome a lot of my fears and inhibition and it has improved my clarity of thought and confidence too."

Sheetal Jain, Healer, PLR Therapist

"With SKY, in a very less time I could focus my concentration and after that I could better meditate, perform any personal and professional activity effectively."

Manish Dua, Professional

"Practicing SKY has changed my life completely. I found the real purpose of my life. From pursuing my business for last eleven years to being into full time professional healing and now a SKY teacher. My journey wasn't so exciting and fulfilling before as it is now."

Arun Jain, PLR Therapist, Certified SKY Teacher

"SKY technique is the proverbial 'magic wand' I stumbled upon two years back and since then, life has never been the same! It has given me the confidence and I have manifested whatever I wished for in my life."

Dr. Poonam Mitra, Practicing Dentist

"SKY is an exciting Discovery! SKY is a 12-minute magic which has helped me to achieve my academic goals, mental peace, confidence. It has also improved my physical health and relationships."

Hiral Joshi, Student, Seeker

The magic of SKY spreads to organisations

"A workshop was conducted on stress management by Mr Santosh Joshi, Founder of SKY Healing Technique at 21 Punjab Unit Location, from 4th to 7th August 2014. The workshop was conducted in a commendable manner which proved to be of great help for all the ranks of the unit. The simple SKY Healing Technique has been very useful and appreciated by all and incorporated in daily routine of the unit."

Col. Manish Rana, Commanding Officer, 21 Punjab Regiment

"We found the workshop informative and worthwhile. You did an outstanding job of sharing your expertise with us. Your commitment to share, listen and support out employees is priceless. Your enthusiasm and positive spirit made our time both productive and fun."

Sanjay Goel, Vice-President-Works, JSW Steel Coated Products Limited

"Our employees who have participated in the SKY workshop have found it to be very useful and instrumental in reducing stress. Participants have shared that they are experiencing physical, emotional, psychological and spiritual benefits after practicing SKY."

Capt. Naresh Kakkar, General Manager-HR, Ranbaxy Laboratories Limited

"Participants in the workshop found it very interesting that a small 12 minutes technique is so effective in reducing stress. Another feedback was that it helped in improving the concentration and made them calmer."

Sanjay Beswal, Director, Andees Impex

"The Sky workshop is a magic elixir which no doctor can prescribe. Santosh's profound knowledge and mastery over the subject, all imparted in the most user friendly format makes SKY a must attend workshop. I came in the SKY workshop as a caterpillar in a cocoon only to leave as happy butterfly."

Anand Shirali, Country Head-Distribution & Sales, Blitz Multimedia Private Limited

"It was a nice experience indeed. To relieve the stress from mechanical way of life with divine way. The ancient way of breathing therapy revived in capsule form tailor made for corporate officials."

Sabyasach dutta, JSW Steel Ltd.